Taste of Home

PUMPKIN

TASTE OF HOME BOOKS • RDA ENTHUSIAST BRANDS, LLC • MILWAUKEE, WI

T004733

Taste of Home

© 2018 RDA Enthusiast Brands, LLC
1610 N. 2nd St. Suite 102
Milwaukee, WI 53212

Visit us at tasteofhome.com
for other *Taste of Home* books
and products.

**International Standard Book
Number:** 978-1-61765-784-9

**Library of Congress Control
Number:** 2018939396

Cover Photographer:
Grace Natoli Sheldon
Set Stylist:
Melissa Franco
Food Stylist:
Kathryn Conrad

Pictured on front cover:
Sausage & Rice Stuffed
Pumpkins, p. 87
Pictured on spine:
Autumn Pumpkin
Cupcakes, p. 123
Pictured on title page:
Sour Cream Pumpkin
Cheesecake, p. 119
**Pictured on back cover
(from left):**
Pumpkin Waffles with
Orange Walnut Butter, p. 7;
Pumpkin Charlotte, p. 197;
Pumpkin Spice Latte, p. 65

Printed in China.
3 5 7 9 10 8 6 4 2

**Spiced Pumpkin
Coffee Shakes
p. 73**

GET SOCIAL WITH US!

To find a recipe tasteofhome.com
To submit a recipe tasteofhome.com/submit
To find out about other *Taste of Home*
products shoptasteofhome.com

LIKE US
facebook.com/
tasteofhome

FOLLOW US
@tasteofhome

TWEET US
twitter.com/
tasteofhome

PIN US
pinterest.com/
taste_of_home

TABLE OF CONTENTS

Pumpkin Lasagna, p. 107
Pretty Pumpkin Cinnamon Buns, p. 32

THE SPICE OF LIFE

From holiday pie to cheesy lasagna, pumpkin flavors a variety of cozy dishes.

CINNAMON
4 tsp.

GINGER
2 tsp.

CLOVES
1 tsp.

NUTMEG
½ tsp.

Customize your blend with these sweet, bright and savory additions:
• Allspice
• Black pepper
• Cardamom
• Fennel seed
• Mace
• Dried lemon peel
• Star aniseed

HOMEMADE PUMPKIN PIE SPICE

Combine all ingredients. Store in an airtight container in a cool, dry place for up to 6 months.

FALL IN LOVE WITH PUMPKIN

Our biggest collection of best-loved pumpkin recipes is brimming with gourd-geous dishes for breakfast, dinner, cocktail hour, snack time and just about every occasion in between.

It wouldn't be fall without a pumpkin-spiced coffee—and our ice cream coffee shake is tasty, tall and so pretty! The next time you entertain, you'll want to break out the blender for these sensationally sweet sips (pictured p. 2).

Take it from us: Even meat lovers adore pumpkin lasagna. If you haven't tasted yet how perfectly pumpkin pairs with rich, salty cheese, hearty sage and pasta (pictured p. 3), you've been missing out!

Fragrant cinnamon rolls hot from the oven will rouse any sleepyhead out of bed. Our pumpkin-based version (pictured p. 3) is kissed with butterscotch and has an irresistible vanilla icing.

Find 100+ sweet and savory dishes that make anytime pumpkin time. Turn the page and discover the magic that pumpkin brings.

Use your homemade pumpkin pie spice in these and 20 other dishes in the book: Fluffy Pumpkin Pancakes, p. 19; Pumpkin Cupcakes with Spiced Frosting, p. 156; Cranberry-Pumpkin Praline Pie, p. 136.

BREAKFAST & BRUNCH

PUMPKIN WAFFLES WITH ORANGE WALNUT BUTTER

This is so delicious! Bring a flourish to the breakfast table with these unique and flavorful waffles.
—BRANDI DAVIS, PULLMAN, WA

TAKES: 30 MIN. • **MAKES:** 4 SERVINGS

- ½ cup butter, softened
- 1 Tbsp. grated orange peel
- ¼ cup chopped walnuts

WAFFLES

- 1 cup plus 2 Tbsp. all-purpose flour
- 2 Tbsp. brown sugar
- 1 tsp. ground cinnamon
- ½ tsp. salt
- ½ tsp. baking powder
- ¼ tsp. baking soda
- 2 large eggs
- 1 cup 2% milk
- ½ cup canned pumpkin
- 2 Tbsp. butter, melted
  Maple syrup

1. Preheat waffle maker. Mix softened butter and orange peel; stir in walnuts.
2. Whisk together the first six waffle ingredients. In another bowl, whisk together eggs, milk, pumpkin and melted butter; add to dry ingredients. Stir just until moistened.
3. Bake waffles according to the manufacturer's directions until golden brown. Serve with butter mixture and maple syrup.

2 WAFFLES WITH 2 TBSP. ORANGE WALNUT BUTTER:
536 cal., 38g fat (20g sat. fat), 174mg chol., 731mg sod., 41g carb. (11g sugars, 3g fiber), 11g pro.

OVERNIGHT PUMPKIN FRENCH TOAST CASSEROLE

Recipes that don't tie me to the kitchen—that's what I'm all about. I like to make this luscious dish the night before breakfast or brunch with guests.

—PATRICIA HARMON, BADEN, PA

PREP: 20 MIN. + CHILLING • **BAKE:** 65 MIN.
MAKES: 12 SERVINGS

- 1 loaf (1 lb.) cinnamon-raisin bread
- 1 pkg. (8 oz.) reduced-fat cream cheese, cut into ¾-in. cubes
- 8 large eggs
- 1 can (12 oz.) evaporated milk
- 1 cup canned pumpkin
- ⅔ cup packed brown sugar
- ½ cup fat-free milk
- 2 tsp. ground cinnamon
- ¼ tsp. ground nutmeg
- ¼ tsp. ground ginger
- ⅛ tsp. ground cloves
- ½ tsp. salt
- ½ cup chopped pecans
  Confectioners' sugar, optional
  Maple syrup, warmed, optional

1. Cut each slice of bread into quarters. Arrange half of the bread in a greased 13x9-in. baking dish; layer with cubed cream cheese and remaining bread, pressing down slightly.

2. In a large bowl, whisk the eggs, evaporated milk, pumpkin, brown sugar, milk, spices and salt. Pour over top. Refrigerate, covered, overnight.

3. Preheat oven to 350°. Remove casserole from refrigerator while oven heats. Bake, covered, for 40 minutes. Uncover; sprinkle with pecans. Bake, uncovered, 25-30 minutes or until lightly browned and a knife inserted in the center comes out clean.

4. Let stand 5-10 minutes before serving. If desired, dust the top with confectioners' sugar and serve with maple syrup.

1 PIECE: 302 cal., 13g fat (6g sat. fat), 148mg chol., 342mg sod., 36g carb. (20g sugars, 4g fiber), 13g pro.

PUMPKIN-PECAN BAKED OATMEAL

Here's a yummy wintertime treat. My husband rarely eats in the morning, but when I make my baked oatmeal, he digs right in.
—**ALEX MUEHL, AUSTIN, TX**

PREP: 15 MIN. + CHILLING • **BAKE:** 30 MIN. • **MAKES:** 6 SERVINGS

- 2 large eggs
- 3 cups quick-cooking oats
- 1 can (15 oz.) solid-pack pumpkin
- 1 cup 2% milk
- ¾ cup packed brown sugar
- ½ cup dried cranberries
- ⅓ cup butter, melted
- 1½ tsp. baking powder
- 1 tsp. vanilla extract
- ½ tsp. ground nutmeg
- ¼ tsp. salt
- ¼ tsp. ground cloves
- ¼ cup chopped pecans
  Additional 2% milk and brown sugar

1. In a large bowl, combine the first 12 ingredients. Transfer to a greased 11x7-in. baking dish. Refrigerate, covered, 8 hours or overnight.
2. Remove oatmeal from refrigerator 30 minutes before baking. Preheat oven to 350°. Uncover and stir oatmeal; sprinkle with pecans. Bake, uncovered, 30-35 minutes or until a thermometer reads 160°. Serve warm with additional milk and brown sugar.

¾ **CUP:** 478 cal., 19g fat (8g sat. fat), 92mg chol., 335mg sod., 71g carb. (39g sugars, 7g fiber), 10g pro.

SAVORY PUMPKIN QUICHE

This quiche satisfies a seasonal craving I get for all things pumpkin. Fresh mushrooms add flavor, and I try different types such as baby portobello and cremini mushrooms.

—RACHEL GARCIA, COLORADO SPRINGS, CO

PREP: 15 MIN. • **BAKE:** 50 MIN. + STANDING
MAKES: 8 SERVINGS

- 3 large eggs
- 1 can (15 oz.) solid-pack pumpkin
- 1 can (5 oz.) evaporated milk
- ½ lb. bacon strips, cooked and crumbled
- ½ cup sliced mushrooms
- ¼ cup finely chopped onion
- ¼ cup finely chopped green pepper
- ½ cup grated Parmesan cheese
- 1 Tbsp. all-purpose flour
- 1 frozen deep-dish pie crust

1. Preheat oven to 375°. In a large bowl, whisk eggs, pumpkin and milk until blended. Stir in bacon, mushrooms, onion and pepper. Toss cheese with flour; stir into egg mixture. Pour into pie crust.
2. Bake on a lower oven rack 50-60 minutes or until a knife inserted in the center comes out clean. Let stand 15 minutes before cutting.

1 SLICE: 231 cal., 13g fat (5g sat. fat), 96mg chol., 417mg sod., 18g carb. (5g sugars, 2g fiber), 11g pro.

HELPFUL HINT
No need to add salt to this savory quiche. The Parmesan cheese and bacon already create plenty of salty flavor.

PUMPKIN CREAM OF WHEAT

TAKES: 10 MIN. • **MAKES:** 1 SERVING

- ½ cup 2% milk
- ¼ cup half-and-half cream
- 3 Tbsp. Cream of Wheat
- ¼ cup canned pumpkin
- 2 tsp. sugar
- ⅛ tsp. ground cinnamon
- Additional 2% milk

In a small microwave-safe bowl, combine the milk, cream and Cream of Wheat. Microwave, uncovered, on high for 1 minute; stir until blended. Cover and cook for 1-2 minutes or until thickened, stirring every 30 seconds. Stir in the pumpkin, sugar and cinnamon. Serve with additional milk.

1 CUP: 314 cal., 9g fat (6g sat. fat), 39mg chol., 96mg sod., 46g carb. (18g sugars, 4g fiber), 10g pro.

"Try an autumn-inspired breakfast that tastes like pumpkin pie…but without the guilt! Double the recipe if you feel like sharing."

—AMY BASHTOVOI, SIDNEY, NE

PUMPKIN-CRANBERRY BREAKFAST BAKE

I love trying new ways to use pumpkin. This bread pudding was a hit with my family for a weekend breakfast.

—TERRI CRANDALL, GARDNERVILLE, NV

PREP: 15 MIN. + CHILLING • **BAKE:** 30 MIN.
MAKES: 12 SERVINGS

- 1 loaf (1 lb.) brioche, cut into 1-in. cubes
- ½ cup dried cranberries
- ½ cup chopped walnuts, toasted
- 2 cups 2% milk
- 1 cup canned pumpkin
- ¾ cup packed brown sugar
- 4 large eggs
- ½ tsp. grated lemon peel
- 2 Tbsp. butter, melted
- 1 tsp. vanilla extract
- 1 tsp. ground cinnamon
- ¼ tsp. ground nutmeg
- ¼ tsp. ground ginger
- ⅛ tsp. ground cloves
  Maple syrup

1. Place bread cubes in a greased 13x9-in. baking dish; sprinkle with cranberries and walnuts. Whisk together the next 11 ingredients until blended; pour over bread. Refrigerate, covered, overnight.

2. Preheat oven to 350°. Remove casserole from refrigerator while oven heats. Bake, uncovered, until puffed, golden and a knife inserted in the center comes out clean, 30-35 minutes. Let stand 5-10 minutes before serving. Serve with syrup.

NOTE To toast nuts, bake in a shallow pan in a 350° oven for 5-10 minutes or cook in a skillet over low heat until lightly browned, stirring occasionally.

1 PIECE: 303 cal., 12g fat (6g sat. fat), 101mg chol., 230mg sod., 43g carb. (26g sugars, 2g fiber), 7g pro.

HELPFUL HINT

Brioche is a bakery bread rich with butter and eggs. Chopped croissants are a great substitute if you can't find brioche. Jewish challah bread, leftover Pumpkin Egg Bread (p. 48), Hawaiian sweet dinner rolls or a blend of these could also be used.

FLUFFY PUMPKIN PANCAKES

My daughters love these tender, fluffy pancakes served with butter, syrup and whipped cream. We freeze the extras—for popping into the toaster.

—MINDY BAUKNECHT, TWO RIVERS, WI

TAKES: 30 MIN. • **MAKES:** 6 PANCAKES

- ⅓ **cup all-purpose flour**
- ⅓ **cup whole wheat flour**
- 2 **Tbsp. sugar**
- ½ **tsp. baking powder**
- ½ **tsp. baking soda**
- ¼ **tsp. pumpkin pie spice**
- ⅛ **tsp. ground cinnamon**
  Dash salt
- 1 **large egg**
- ½ **cup fat-free milk**
- ⅓ **cup vanilla yogurt**
- ⅓ **cup canned pumpkin**
- 1 **Tbsp. canola oil**
- ⅛ **tsp. vanilla extract**
  Maple syrup

1. In a bowl, whisk together the first eight ingredients. In another bowl, whisk the next six ingredients until blended. Add to dry ingredients; stir just until moistened.

2. Lightly coat a griddle with cooking spray; preheat over medium heat. Pour batter by ⅓ cupfuls onto griddle. Cook until bubbles on top begin to pop. Turn; cook until golden brown. Serve with syrup.

3 PANCAKES: 360 cal., 11g fat (2g sat. fat), 109mg chol., 579mg sod., 55g carb. (23g sugars, 5g fiber), 13g pro.

PRESSURE COOKER PUMPKIN SPICE OATMEAL

There's nothing like a bowl of warm oatmeal in the morning, and my spiced version works in a pressure cooker. Store leftovers in the fridge.

—JORDAN MASON, BROOKVILLE, PA

....

TAKES: 30 MIN. • **MAKES:** 6 SERVINGS

- 1¼ cups steel-cut oats
- 3 Tbsp. brown sugar
- 1½ tsp. pumpkin pie spice
- 1 tsp. ground cinnamon
- ¾ tsp. salt
- 3 cups water
- 1½ cups 2% milk
- 1 can (15 oz.) solid-pack pumpkin
  Optional toppings: toasted chopped pecans, ground cinnamon, additional brown sugar and 2% milk

1. Stir together the first seven ingredients in a 6-qt. electric pressure cooker. Lock lid; make sure vent is closed. Select manual setting; adjust pressure to high and set time for 10 minutes.

2. When finished cooking, allow the pressure to naturally release for 10 minutes, then quick-release any remaining pressure according to manufacturer's directions. Stir in pumpkin; let stand 5-10 minutes to thicken. Serve with toppings as desired.

NOTE Steel-cut oats are also known as Scotch oats or Irish oatmeal.

1 CUP: 208 cal., 4g fat (1g sat. fat), 5mg chol., 329mg sod., 39g carb. (13g sugars, 6g fiber), 7g pro.

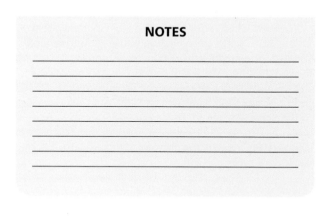

NOTES

SPICED PUMPKIN FRENCH TOAST CASSEROLE

I make this breakfast dish anytime, but it's especially perfect for the holidays. Make it the evening before, so it is ready to bake in the morning. Breakfast is a breeze!

—JOANNE WESSEL, GREENWOOD, IN

PREP: 20 MIN. + CHILLING • **BAKE:** 65 MIN. • **MAKES:** 12 SERVINGS

- 8 large eggs
- 2 cups whole milk
- 2 cups heavy whipping cream
- 1 can (15 oz.) solid-pack pumpkin
- 1½ cups sugar
- 2 tsp. vanilla extract
- 1½ tsp. ground cinnamon
- ½ tsp. salt
- ½ tsp. ground ginger
- ¼ tsp. ground nutmeg
- 14 cups cubed challah or egg bread (about 28 oz.)
- ½ cup raisins
  Confectioners' sugar and maple syrup, optional

1. In a large bowl, whisk the first 10 ingredients until blended. Add bread cubes and raisins; gently stir to combine. Transfer to a greased 13x9-in. baking dish. Refrigerate, covered, several hours or overnight.
2. Preheat oven to 350°. Remove casserole from refrigerator while oven heats. Bake, uncovered, 65-75 minutes or until edges of bread are golden brown and a knife inserted in the center comes out clean.
3. Let stand 5-10 minutes before serving. If desired, serve with confectioners' sugar and syrup.

1 SERVING: 529 cal., 23g fat (12g sat. fat), 207mg chol., 428mg sod., 68g carb. (34g sugars, 3g fiber), 13g pro.

PUMPKIN PIE-SPICED GRANOLA

My husband says this granola with pumpkin and spices tastes like a bite of real pumpkin pie, and it's a whole lot quicker to make.

—SARAH OZIMEK, OCONOMOWOC, WI

PREP: 15 MIN. • **BAKE:** 40 MIN. + COOLING
MAKES: 4 CUPS

- 4 cups old-fashioned oats
- 1 cup raw pumpkin seeds or pepitas
- 1 cup canned pumpkin
- ½ cup packed brown sugar
- ¼ cup honey
- ¼ cup canola oil
- 2 Tbsp. water
- 2 tsp. ground cinnamon
- ¾ tsp. salt
- ¾ tsp. ground ginger
- ¾ tsp. ground nutmeg
- ¼ tsp. ground cloves

1. Preheat oven to 325°. In a large bowl, combine oats and pumpkin seeds. In a small saucepan, whisk remaining ingredients; bring to a boil. Remove from heat. Pour over oat mixture; toss to coat.
2. Spread evenly into two greased 15x10x1-in. baking pans. Bake 40-50 minutes or until golden brown, stirring every 10 minutes. Cool completely on wire racks. Store in an airtight container.

½ **CUP:** 395 cal., 17g fat (2g sat. fat), 0 chol., 265mg sod., 55g carb. (24g sugars, 6g fiber), 10g pro.

HELPFUL HINT
You can make your own pancake mix for this recipe with 2 cups plus 1½ Tbsp. flour, 2 Tbsp. sugar and 4¼ tsp. baking powder.

CHOCOLATE CHIP-PUMPKIN PANCAKES

Who can resist a sky-high stack of golden, fluffy pancakes? Pumpkin and chocolate chips take them over the top!
—**ELIZABETH GODECKE, CHICAGO, IL**

PREP: 15 MIN. • **COOK:** 5 MIN./BATCH • **MAKES:** 15 PANCAKES

2⅓ cups pancake mix
½ tsp. ground cinnamon
¼ tsp. ground nutmeg
¼ tsp. ground cloves
2 large eggs
1¼ cups buttermilk
⅓ cup canned pumpkin
¼ cup butter, melted
1 Tbsp. honey
½ cup miniature semisweet chocolate chips
    Additional miniature semisweet chocolate chips and honey

1. In a large bowl, combine pancake mix, cinnamon, nutmeg and cloves. In a small bowl, whisk eggs, buttermilk, pumpkin, butter and honey; stir into the dry ingredients just until moistened. Fold in chocolate chips.

2. Lightly grease a griddle; heat over medium heat. Pour batter by ¼ cupfuls onto griddle. Cook until bubbles on top begin to pop and bottoms are golden brown. Turn; cook until second side is golden brown. Serve with additional chocolate chips and honey.

3 PANCAKES: 422 cal., 18g fat (10g sat. fat), 111mg chol., 844mg sod., 57g carb. (18g sugars, 5g fiber), 11g pro.

AUTUMN POWER PORRIDGE

PREP: 15 MIN. • **COOK:** 30 MIN. • **MAKES:** 4 SERVINGS

- 3 cups water
- ¾ cup steel-cut oats
- ½ cup quinoa, rinsed
- ¼ tsp. salt
- ¾ cup canned pumpkin
- 1 tsp. pumpkin pie spice
- 3 Tbsp. agave nectar or maple syrup
- ½ cup dried cranberries
- ⅓ cup coarsely chopped walnuts, toasted
  Milk

1. In a large saucepan, combine the water, oats, quinoa and salt. Bring to a boil. Reduce heat; cover and simmer for 20 minutes.

2. Stir in the pumpkin, pie spice and agave nectar. Remove from the heat; cover and let mixture stand for 5 minutes or until water is absorbed and grains are tender. Stir in cranberries and walnuts. Serve with milk if desired.

NOTE Steel-cut oats are also known as Scotch oats or Irish oatmeal.

1 CUP: 361 cal., 10g fat (1g sat. fat), 0 chol., 155mg sod., 65g carb. 24g sugars, 7g fiber), 9g pro.

"This rib-sticking porridge is made with oats and protein-rich quinoa. Pumpkin, maple syrup, walnuts and dried cranberries make it a delicious and kid-friendly breakfast."

—JENNIFER WICKES, PINE BEACH, NJ

**BREADS &
MUFFINS**

PUMPKIN-APPLE MUFFINS WITH STREUSEL TOPPING

My mother always made these tasty muffins when our family got together at her house. Now they're a family favorite at my house, and my in-laws love them, too!

—CAROLYN RILEY, CARLISLE, PA

PREP: 20 MIN. • **BAKE:** 30 MIN. + COOLING
MAKES: 1½ DOZEN

- 2½ cups all-purpose flour
- 2 cups sugar
- 1 Tbsp. pumpkin pie spice
- 1 tsp. baking soda
- ½ tsp. salt
- 2 large eggs, lightly beaten
- 1 cup canned pumpkin
- ½ cup vegetable oil
- 2 cups finely chopped peeled apples

TOPPING

- ¼ cup sugar
- 2 Tbsp. all-purpose flour
- ½ tsp. ground cinnamon
- 1 Tbsp. butter or margarine

In a large bowl, combine flour, sugar, pumpkin pie spice, baking soda and salt. Combine eggs, pumpkin and oil; stir into dry ingredients just until moistened. Fold in apples. Fill greased or paper-lined muffin cups three-fourths full. For topping, combine sugar, flour and cinnamon. Cut in butter until mixture resembles coarse crumbs; sprinkle 1 tsp. over each muffin. Bake in a 350° oven until muffins test done, 30-35 minutes. Cool in pan 10 minutes before removing to a wire rack.

1 MUFFIN: 243 cal., 8g fat (1g sat. fat), 25mg chol., 150mg sod., 42g carb. (27g sugars, 1g fiber), 3g pro.

PRETTY PUMPKIN CINNAMON BUNS

I make sticky buns and cinnamon rolls quite often because my husband loves them. One day, I had some fresh pumpkin on hand and decided to try pumpkin cinnamon buns. We loved the results!

—GLENDA JOSEPH, CHAMBERSBURG, PA

PREP: 45 MIN. + RISING • **BAKE:** 25 MIN.
MAKES: 2 DOZEN

- 2 Tbsp. active dry yeast
- ½ cup warm water (110° to 115°)
- 4 large eggs
- 1 cup shortening
- 1 cup canned pumpkin
- 1 cup warm whole milk (110° to 115°)
- ½ cup sugar
- ½ cup packed brown sugar
- ⅓ cup instant vanilla pudding mix
- ⅓ cup instant butterscotch pudding mix
- 1 tsp. salt
- 8 to 9 cups all-purpose flour

FILLING

- ¼ cup butter, melted
- 1 cup packed brown sugar
- 2 tsp. ground cinnamon

ICING

- 3 Tbsp. water
- 2 Tbsp. butter, softened
- 1 tsp. ground cinnamon
- 2 cups confectioners' sugar
- 1½ tsp. vanilla extract

1. In a large bowl, dissolve yeast in warm water. Add eggs, shortening, pumpkin, milk, sugars, pudding mixes, salt and 6 cups flour. Beat until smooth. Stir in enough remaining flour to form a soft dough (dough will be sticky).

2. Turn onto a floured surface; knead until smooth and elastic, 6-8 minutes. Place in a greased bowl, turning once to grease top. Cover and let rise in a warm place until doubled, about 1 hour.

3. Punch the dough down; divide in half. Roll each portion into a 12x8-in. rectangle; brush with melted butter. Combine brown sugar and cinnamon; sprinkle over dough to within ½ in. of edges.

4. Roll up jelly-roll style, starting with a long side; pinch seams to seal. Cut each roll into 12 slices. Place cut side down in two greased 13x9-in. baking pans. Cover and let rise until doubled, about 30 minutes.

5. Bake at 350° for 22-28 minutes or until golden brown. In a small bowl, combine water, butter and cinnamon. Add confectioners' sugar and vanilla; beat until smooth. Spread over buns. Serve warm.

1 BUN: 399 cal., 13g fat (4g sat. fat), 40mg chol., 188mg sod., 65g carb. (31g sugars, 2g fiber), 6g pro.

CONTEST-WINNING CHOCOLATE CHIP PUMPKIN BREAD

A touch of cinnamon helps blend the chocolate and pumpkin flavors in this tender bread. And since the recipe makes two loaves, you can send one to a bake sale and keep one at home for your family to enjoy.

—LORA STANLEY, BENNINGTON, KS

PREP: 15 MIN. • **BAKE:** 1 HOUR + COOLING
MAKES: 2 LOAVES (16 SLICES EACH)

- 3 cups all-purpose flour
- 2 tsp. ground cinnamon
- 1 tsp. salt
- 1 tsp. baking soda
- 4 large eggs
- 2 cups sugar
- 2 cups canned pumpkin
- 1½ cups canola oil
- 1½ cups semisweet chocolate chips

1. In a large bowl, combine flour, cinnamon, salt and baking soda. In another bowl, beat the eggs, sugar, pumpkin and oil. Stir into dry ingredients just until moistened. Fold in the chocolate chips.

2. Pour into two greased 8x4-in. loaf pans. Bake at 350° for 60-70 minutes or until a toothpick inserted in the center comes out clean. Cool for 10 minutes before removing from pans to wire racks.

1 SLICE: 234 cal., 13g fat (3g sat. fat), 27mg chol., 123mg sod., 28g carb. (17g sugars, 1g fiber), 3g pro.

PUMPKIN GINGER SCONES

I made these lovely scones one day when I was looking for a way to use up leftover pumpkin, and I was not disappointed. I often use my food processor to stir up the dough just until it comes together. It's so simple to prepare this way.

—BRENDA JACKSON, GARDEN CITY, KS

TAKES: 30 MIN. • **MAKES:** 8 SCONES

- 2 cups all-purpose flour
- 7 Tbsp. plus 1 tsp. sugar, divided
- 2 tsp. baking powder
- 1 tsp. ground cinnamon
- ½ tsp. salt
- ½ tsp. ground ginger
- ¼ tsp. baking soda
- 5 Tbsp. cold butter, divided
- 1 large egg, lightly beaten
- ¼ cup canned pumpkin
- ¼ cup sour cream

1. In a large bowl, combine flour, 7 Tbsp. sugar, baking powder, cinnamon, salt, ginger and baking soda. Cut in 4 Tbsp. butter until mixture resembles coarse crumbs. Combine the egg, pumpkin and sour cream; stir into dry ingredients just until moistened.

2. Turn onto a floured surface; knead 10 times. Pat into an 8-in. circle. Cut into eight wedges. Separate wedges and place on a greased baking sheet. Melt remaining butter; brush over dough. Sprinkle with remaining sugar.

3. Bake at 425° for 15-20 minutes or until golden brown. Serve warm.

1 SCONE: 249 cal., 9g fat (6g sat. fat), 51mg chol., 372mg sod., 36g carb. (12g sugars, 1g fiber), 4g pro.

PUMPKIN CHIP MUFFINS

PREP: 20 MIN. • **BAKE:** 15 MIN. + COOLING
MAKES: 2 DOZEN

- 4 **large eggs**
- 2 **cups sugar**
- 1 **can (15 oz.) solid-pack pumpkin**
- 1½ **cups canola oil**
- 3 **cups all-purpose flour**
- 2 **tsp. baking soda**
- 1 **tsp. baking powder**
- 1 **tsp. ground cinnamon**
- 1 **tsp. salt**
- 2 **cups semisweet chocolate chips**

1. In a large bowl, beat the eggs, sugar, pumpkin and oil until smooth. Combine the flour, baking soda, baking powder, cinnamon and salt; gradually add to pumpkin mixture and mix well. Fold in chocolate chips. Fill greased or paper-lined muffin cups three-fourths full.
2. Bake at 400° for 15-18 minutes or until a toothpick inserted in the center comes out clean. Cool in pan for 10 minutes before removing to a wire rack.

1 MUFFIN: 328 cal., 19g fat (4g sat. fat), 35mg chol., 250mg sod., 39g carb. (25g sugars, 2g fiber), 4g pro.

My sisters, brothers and I started cooking and baking when we were young. Mom was a very good teacher—she told us we would learn our way around the kitchen. Now, I tell my kids the same thing!

—CINDY MIDDLETON, CHAMPION, AB

PUMPKIN EGGNOG ROLLS

I needed to use up some eggnog, so I swapped it for milk in my sweet roll recipe. Even people who usually don't go for eggnog go back for seconds of these yummy treats.

—REBECCA SOSKE, DOUGLAS, WY

PREP: 40 MIN. + RISING • **BAKE:** 20 MIN.
MAKES: 1 DOZEN

- ½ **cup sugar**
- 1 **pkg. (¼ oz.) active dry yeast**
- ½ **tsp. salt**
- 4½ **cups all-purpose flour**
- ¾ **cup eggnog**
- ½ **cup butter, cubed**
- ¼ **cup canned pumpkin**
- 2 **large eggs**

FILLING

- ½ **cup sugar**
- 1 **tsp. ground cardamom**
- 1 **tsp. ground allspice**
- ¼ **cup butter, melted**

FROSTING

- 2 **oz. cream cheese, softened**
- 2 **Tbsp. eggnog**
- 1 **Tbsp. canned pumpkin**
- ¼ **tsp. ground cardamom**
- 2 **cups confectioners' sugar**

1. In a large bowl, mix sugar, yeast, salt and 2 cups of flour. In a small saucepan, heat eggnog, butter and pumpkin to 120°-130°. Add to dry ingredients; beat on medium speed 2 minutes. Add eggs; beat on high for 2 more minutes. Stir in enough of the remaining flour to form a firm dough.

2. Turn dough onto a floured surface; knead until smooth and elastic, 6-8 minutes. Place in a greased bowl, turning once to grease the top. Cover and let rise in a warm place until doubled, about 1 hour.

3. In a small bowl, mix the sugar, cardamom and allspice. Punch dough down. Turn onto a lightly floured surface and roll into an 18x12-in. rectangle. Brush with melted butter to within ½ in. of edges; sprinkle with sugar mixture. Roll up jelly-roll style, starting with a long side; pinch seam to seal. Cut into 12 slices.

4. Place in a greased 13x9-in. baking pan, cut side down. Cover with a kitchen towel; let rise in a warm place until doubled, about 45 minutes. Preheat oven to 350°. Bake rolls for 20-25 minutes or until golden brown.

5. In a small bowl, beat the cream cheese, eggnog, pumpkin and cardamom until blended. Gradually beat in confectioners' sugar; beat until smooth. Spread over warm rolls.

NOTE This recipe was tested with commercially prepared eggnog.

1 ROLL: 472 cal., 16g fat (9g sat. fat), 81mg chol., 216mg sod., 76g carb. (38g sugars, 2g fiber), 7g pro.

PUMPKIN KNOT ROLLS

These rolls are the lightest, most delicious ones I've ever tasted, and everyone else seems to agree. The pumpkin gives them mild flavor, moist texture and a pretty golden color. At our house, it wouldn't be the holidays without them.

—DIANNA SHIMIZU, ISSAQUAH, WA

PREP: 30 MIN. + RISING • **BAKE:** 15 MIN.
MAKES: 2 DOZEN

- 2 pkg. (¼ oz. each) active dry yeast
- 1 cup warm whole milk (110° to 115°)
- ⅓ cup butter, softened
- ½ cup sugar
- 1 cup canned pumpkin
- 3 large eggs, divided use
- 1½ tsp. salt
- 5½ to 6 cups all-purpose flour
- 1 Tbsp. cold water
  Sesame or poppy seeds, optional

1. In a large bowl, dissolve yeast in warm milk. Add the butter, sugar, pumpkin, 2 eggs, salt and 3 cups of flour. Beat until smooth. Stir in enough remaining flour to form a soft dough. Turn onto a lightly floured surface; knead until smooth and elastic, 6-8 minutes. Place in a greased bowl, turning once to grease top. Cover and let rise in a warm place until doubled, about 1 hour.

2. Punch dough down. Turn onto a lightly floured surface; divide in half. Shape each portion into 12 balls. Roll each ball into a 10-in. rope; tie into a knot and tuck ends under. Place 2 in. apart on greased baking sheets. Cover and let rise until doubled, about 30 minutes.

3. Beat water and remaining egg; brush over rolls. Sprinkle tops with sesame or poppy seeds if desired. Bake at 350° for 15-17 minutes or until golden brown. Remove from pans to wire racks to cool.

1 ROLL: 165 cal., 4g fat (2g sat. fat), 35mg chol., 188mg sod., 28g carb. (5g sugars, 1g fiber), 5g pro.

CRANBERRY PUMPKIN BREAD

Put leftover cranberries and pumpkin to great use in this moist quick bread. It's very good with turkey casserole for an after-Thanksgiving meal.

—DIXIE TERRY, GOREVILLE, IL

PREP: 20 MIN. • **BAKE:** 70 MIN. + COOLING
MAKES: 2 LOAVES (16 SLICES EACH)

- 3¾ cups all-purpose flour
- 3 cups sugar
- 4 tsp. pumpkin pie spice
- 2 tsp. baking soda
- 1 tsp. salt
- 4 large eggs
- 1 can (15 oz.) solid-pack pumpkin
- ½ cup canola oil
- 2 cups fresh or frozen cranberries, thawed
- 1 cup chopped walnuts

1. In a large bowl, combine flour, sugar, pumpkin pie spice, baking soda and salt. In another bowl, whisk the eggs, pumpkin and oil; stir into dry ingredients just until moistened. Fold in cranberries and walnuts.

2. Transfer batter to two greased 9x5-in. loaf pans. Bake at 350° for 70-80 minutes or until a toothpick inserted in the center comes out clean. Cool for 10 minutes before removing from pans to wire racks to cool completely.

1 SLICE: 197 cal., 6g fat (1g sat. fat), 27mg chol., 162mg sod., 32g carb. (19g sugars, 1g fiber), 4g pro.

PUMPKIN PAN ROLLS

Serve these spicy-sweet pumpkin rolls for dinner—or any time of day—and get ready to hear a chorus of yums in your kitchen!

—LINNEA REIN, TOPEKA, KS

PREP: 20 MIN. + RISING • **BAKE:** 20 MIN.
MAKES: 20 ROLLS

- ¾ **cup whole milk**
- ⅓ **cup packed brown sugar**
- 5 **Tbsp. butter, divided**
- 1 **tsp. salt**
- 2 **pkg. (¼ oz. each) active dry yeast**
- ½ **cup warm water (110° to 115°)**
- 2 **to 2½ cups all-purpose flour**
- 1½ **cups whole wheat flour**
- ½ **cup canned pumpkin**
- ½ **tsp. ground cinnamon**
- ¼ **tsp. ground ginger**
- ¼ **tsp. ground nutmeg**

1. In a small saucepan, heat the milk, brown sugar, 4 Tbsp. butter and salt to 110°-115°; set aside.

2. In a large bowl, dissolve yeast in warm water. Stir in milk mixture. Add 1½ cups all-purpose flour, whole wheat flour, pumpkin and spices. Beat until smooth. Add enough remaining all-purpose flour to form a soft dough.

3. Turn onto a floured surface; knead until smooth and elastic, 6-8 minutes. Place in a greased bowl, turning once to grease top. Cover; let rise in a warm place until doubled, about 1 hour.

4. Punch dough down. Divide into 20 pieces; shape into balls. Place in a greased 13x9-in. baking pan. Cover rolls and let rise for 30 minutes or until doubled.

5. Preheat oven to 375°. Melt the remaining butter; brush over dough. Bake 20-25 minutes or until golden brown. Remove from pan to a wire rack. Serve warm.

1 ROLL: 124 cal., 3g fat (2g sat. fat), 9mg chol., 154mg sod., 21g carb. (5g sugars, 2g fiber), 3g pro. **DIABETIC EXCHANGES:** 1½ starch, ½ fat.

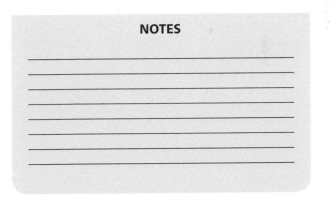

NOTES

PUMPKIN EGG BRAID

I created this bread to celebrate our two favorite holidays, Thanksgiving and Hanukkah. Try it with flavored butters, and use the leftovers for French toast or sandwiches.

—SARA MELLAS, HARTFORD, CT

PREP: 30 MIN. + RISING • **BAKE:** 20 MIN.
MAKES: 1 LOAF (12 SLICES)

- 1 pkg. (¼ oz.) active dry yeast
- 3 Tbsp. warm water (110° to 115°)
- ½ cup canned pumpkin
- 1 large egg
- 2 Tbsp. brown sugar
- 2 Tbsp. butter, softened
- 1 tsp. pumpkin pie spice
- ½ tsp. salt
- 2 to 2½ cups bread flour

EGG WASH

- 1 large egg
- 1 Tbsp. water

HELPFUL HINT

For pretty results, start braiding bread at the center of the loaf and work your way out to the ends. This ensures an even shape.

1. In a small bowl, dissolve the yeast in warm water. In a large bowl, combine pumpkin, egg, brown sugar, butter, pie spice, salt, yeast mixture and 1 cup flour; beat on medium speed until smooth. Stir in enough remaining flour to form a soft dough. (The dough will be sticky.)

2. Turn the dough onto a floured surface; knead until smooth and elastic, 6-8 minutes. Place in a greased bowl, turning once to grease the top. Cover and let rise in a warm place until doubled, about 1 hour.

3. Punch down dough. Turn onto a lightly floured surface; divide into thirds. Roll each into a 16-in. rope. Place ropes on a greased baking sheet and braid. Pinch ends to seal; tuck under.

4. Cover bread with a kitchen towel; let rise in a warm place until almost doubled, about 45 minutes. Preheat oven to 350°.

5. For egg wash, in a small bowl, whisk egg and water until blended; brush over loaf. Bake 20-25 minutes or until golden brown. Remove from pan to a wire rack to cool.

1 SLICE: 126 cal., 3g fat (2g sat. fat), 36mg chol., 129mg sod., 20g carb. (3g sugars, 1g fiber), 4g pro. **DIABETIC EXCHANGES:** 1 starch, ½ fat.

PUMPKIN SURPRISE MUFFINS

Filled with cream cheese and apricot preserves, these almond-topped pumpkin muffins are heavenly.

—ELIZABETH BLONDEFIELD, SAN JOSE, CA

PREP: 20 MIN. • **BAKE:** 20 MIN. • **MAKES:** 14 MUFFINS

- 2 cups all-purpose flour
- 1 Tbsp. baking powder
- 1 tsp. ground cinnamon
- ¼ tsp. salt
- ¼ tsp. ground ginger
- ¼ tsp. ground nutmeg
- ½ cup plus 3 Tbsp. sugar, divided
- 2 large eggs
- 1 cup canned pumpkin
- ½ cup sour cream
- 6 Tbsp. butter, melted
- 7 Tbsp. apricot preserves
- 4 oz. cream cheese, divided into 14 portions
- ¼ cup sliced almonds

1. Preheat oven to 400°. Whisk together the first six ingredients and ½ cup sugar. In another bowl, whisk eggs, pumpkin, sour cream, melted butter and 3 Tbsp. preserves until blended. Add to flour mixture; stir just until moistened.

2. Fill greased or paper-lined muffin cups half full with batter. Place a portion of cream cheese and about ¾ tsp. preserves in each muffin; cover with remaining batter. Sprinkle with almonds and remaining sugar.

3. Bake muffins until top springs back when touched, 20-25 minutes. Cool 5 minutes before removing from pans to a wire rack. Refrigerate leftovers.

1 MUFFIN: 243 cal., 11g fat (6g sat. fat), 50mg chol., 228mg sod., 33g carb. (16g sugars, 1g fiber), 4g pro.

SWIRLED PUMPKIN YEAST BREAD

I call this my hostess-gift bread, but it's fantastic for any occasion at all. Swirls of cinnamon sugar make every slice irresistible.

—SHIRLEY RUNKLE, ST. PARIS, OH

PREP: 45 MIN. + RISING
BAKE: 50 MIN. + COOLING
MAKES: 2 LOAVES (16 SLICES EACH)

- 3 cups whole wheat flour
- 2 cups quick-cooking oats
- ⅔ cup packed brown sugar
- 2 pkg. (¼ oz. each) active dry yeast
- 2½ tsp. pumpkin pie spice
- 1½ tsp. salt
- 1 tsp. sugar
- 4½ to 5 cups all-purpose flour
- 1½ cups warm water (120° to 130°)
- 1 cup canned pumpkin
- ⅓ cup canola oil
- ⅓ cup unsweetened applesauce
- 2 large eggs
- ½ cup raisins

FILLING

- ½ cup packed brown sugar
- 1 tsp. ground cinnamon
- ¼ cup butter, softened

1. In a large bowl, mix the first seven ingredients and 2 cups all-purpose flour. In a small saucepan, heat water, pumpkin, canola oil and applesauce to 120°-130°. Add to dry ingredients; beat on medium speed for 2 minutes. Add the eggs; beat on high for 2 more minutes. Stir in raisins and enough remaining all-purpose flour to form a firm dough.

2. Turn the dough onto a floured surface; knead until smooth and elastic, 6-8 minutes. Place in a greased bowl, turning once to grease the top. Cover and let rise in a warm place until doubled, about 1 hour.

3. Mix brown sugar and cinnamon. Punch down dough. Turn onto a lightly floured surface; divide in half. Roll each portion into an 18x9-in. rectangle. Spread each with 2 Tbsp. butter to within ½ in. of edges and sprinkle with ¼ cup of the brown sugar mixture. Roll up jelly-roll style, starting with a short side; pinch seam to seal. Place in greased 9x5-in. loaf pans, seam side down. Cover with kitchen towels; let dough rise in a warm place until doubled, about 30 minutes. Preheat oven to 350°.

4. Bake bread until golden brown, 50-60 minutes. Cool 10 minutes before removing from pans to wire racks to cool.

1 SLICE: 202 cal., 5g fat (1g sat. fat), 15mg chol., 130mg sod., 36g carb. (10g sugars, 3g fiber), 5g pro.

RAISIN-FILLED PUMPKIN SPICE BREAD

PREP: 20 MIN. • **BAKE:** 1 HOUR + COOLING
MAKES: 2 LOAVES (16 SLICES EACH)

2½ cups all-purpose flour
2 tsp. baking soda
1 tsp. salt
1 tsp. ground cinnamon
1 tsp. ground nutmeg
3 cups sugar
1 cup canola oil
4 large eggs, beaten
¾ cup buttermilk
1 tsp. vanilla extract
1 tsp. butter flavoring
1 can (15 oz.) solid-pack pumpkin
1 cup raisins
1 cup chopped pecans

In a large bowl, sift together flour, soda, salt, cinnamon and nutmeg. Add sugar, oil, eggs and buttermilk. Mix well. Stir in the flavorings, pumpkin, raisins and pecans. Pour into two greased 9x5-in. loaf pans. Bake at 350° for 60-65 minutes or until bread tests done. Let stand for 10 minutes before removing from pans. Cool on a wire rack.

1 SLICE: 225 cal., 10g fat (1g sat. fat), 27mg chol., 168mg sod., 32g carb. (22g sugars, 1g fiber), 3g pro.

One of the best cooks in our church gave me this recipe years ago. Bake it ahead of time and keep it in the freezer until you need a last-minute gift or potluck item.

—MARTHA SUE STROUD, CLARKSVILLE, TX

PUMPKIN-CRANBERRY CAKE DOUGHNUTS

Pumpkin and cranberry make perfect partners in these tender, spice-filled doughnuts. They're so delicious, you'll be tempted to make them all the time!

—CAROLYN COPE, ALLSTON, MD

PREP: 40 MIN. + CHILLING
COOK: 5 MIN./BATCH
MAKES: 1½ DOZEN

- 3 Tbsp. butter, softened
- 1 cup sugar
- 2 large eggs
- 1 tsp. vanilla extract
- 3½ cups all-purpose flour
- 2 tsp. baking powder
- 1 tsp. salt
- 1 tsp. ground cinnamon
- ½ tsp. baking soda
- ½ tsp. ground ginger
- ¼ tsp. ground cloves
- ⅛ tsp. ground nutmeg
- 1 cup canned pumpkin
- ½ cup buttermilk
- 2 cups fresh or frozen cranberries, coarsely chopped
  Oil for deep-fat frying

SPICED SUGAR

- 1 cup sugar
- ¾ tsp. ground cinnamon
- ¼ tsp. ground ginger
- ⅛ tsp. ground cloves
  Dash ground nutmeg

1. In a large bowl, beat butter and sugar until crumbly, about 2 minutes. Add eggs, one at a time, beating well after each addition. Beat in vanilla.

2. Combine flour, baking powder, salt, cinnamon, baking soda, ginger, cloves and nutmeg. Combine the pumpkin and buttermilk. Add flour mixture to the creamed mixture alternately with buttermilk mixture, beating well after each addition. Stir in the chopped cranberries. Cover and refrigerate overnight.

3. Turn dough onto a lightly floured surface; roll to ½-in. thickness. Cut with a floured 2½-in. doughnut cutter. Reroll the scraps.

4. In an electric skillet or deep fryer, heat oil to 375°. Fry the doughnuts, a few at a time, until golden brown on both sides. Drain on paper towels. In a shallow bowl, combine sugar, cinnamon, ginger, cloves and nutmeg; roll warm doughnuts in mixture before serving.

1 DOUGHNUT: 217 cal., 3g fat (1g sat. fat), 29mg chol., 240mg sod., 44g carb. (24g sugars, 2g fiber), 4g pro.

SLOW COOKER PUMPKIN YEAST BREAD

Savor the rich flavors of fall with this homey loaf that you can bake up in the slow cooker. Butterscotch chips add a sweet surprise.

—ERICA POLLY, SUN PRAIRIE, WI

PREP: 20 MIN. • **COOK:** 2½ HOURS + COOLING
MAKES: 1 LOAF (12 SLICES)

⅓ cup packed brown sugar
1 pkg. (¼ oz.) quick-rise yeast
2 tsp. pumpkin pie spice
¾ tsp. salt
3½ to 4 cups all-purpose flour
¾ cup 2% milk
2 Tbsp. butter, cubed
¾ cup canned pumpkin
1 large egg, lightly beaten
⅓ cup raisins
⅓ cup chopped pecans, toasted
⅓ cup butterscotch chips, optional

1. In a large bowl, mix brown sugar, yeast, pie spice, salt and 1½ cups flour. In a small saucepan, heat milk and butter to 120°-130°; stir into dry ingredients. Stir in the pumpkin, egg and enough remaining flour to form a soft dough (dough will be sticky).

2. Turn dough onto a floured surface; knead until smooth and elastic, 6-8 minutes. During the last few minutes of kneading, add raisins, pecans and, if desired, butterscotch chips. Shape into a 6-in. round loaf; transfer to a greased double thickness of heavy-duty foil (about 12 in. square). Lifting with foil, place in a 6-qt. slow cooker. Press the foil against the bottom and sides of the slow cooker.

3. Cook bread, covered, on high for 2½-3 hours or until a thermometer reads 190°-200°. Remove to a wire rack and cool completely before slicing.

1 SLICE: 228 cal., 5g fat (2g sat. fat), 22mg chol., 180mg sod., 40g carb. (10g sugars, 2g fiber), 6g pro.

PUMPKIN OAT MUFFINS

It isn't Thanksgiving or Christmas in my house until these are on the table! Enjoy the flavors of pumpkin pie in easy-to-eat muffin form.
—CAROL HALE, SARVER, PA

PREP: 15 MIN. • **BAKE:** 15 MIN. • **MAKES:** 1 DOZEN

- 1 cup all-purpose flour
- ½ cup packed brown sugar
- 2 tsp. baking powder
- 1 tsp. pumpkin pie spice
- ½ tsp. salt
- ¼ tsp. baking soda
- 1 large egg, lightly beaten
- ¾ cup canned pumpkin
- ¼ cup whole milk
- ¼ cup canola oil
- 1 cup old-fashioned oats
- ½ cup raisins

TOPPING
- ⅓ cup packed brown sugar
- 1 Tbsp. all-purpose flour
- ¾ tsp. pumpkin pie spice
- 1 Tbsp. cold butter

1. In a large bowl, combine first six ingredients. Combine the egg, pumpkin, milk and oil; add to the dry ingredients just until moistened. Stir in the oats and raisins.

2. Fill greased or paper-lined muffin cups two-thirds full. In a small bowl, combine brown sugar, flour and pie spice; cut in butter until crumbly. Sprinkle 1 rounded teaspoonful over each muffin. Bake at 375° for 15-20 minutes or until a toothpick comes out clean.

3. Cool for 5 minutes before removing from pan to a wire rack. Serve warm.

1 MUFFIN: 204 cal., 7g fat (2g sat. fat), 21mg chol., 214mg sod., 34g carb. (19g sugars, 2g fiber), 3g pro.

STREUSEL PUMPKIN SWEET ROLLS

My sons love anything pumpkin—including these fragrant and irresistible sweet rolls.
—JULIE FEHR, MARTENSVILLE, SK

PREP: 45 MIN. + RISING • **BAKE:** 20 MIN.
MAKES: 2 DOZEN

  1 **pkg. (¼ oz.) active dry yeast**
1¼ **cups warm 2% milk (110° to 115°)**
  1 **cup solid-pack pumpkin**
  ½ **cup sugar**
  ½ **cup butter, melted**
  1 **tsp. salt**
4¾ to 5¾ **cups all-purpose flour**
STREUSEL
1½ **cups all-purpose flour**
  1 **cup packed brown sugar**
  1 **tsp. ground cinnamon**
  ½ **tsp. ground allspice**
  ¾ **cup cold butter, cubed**
GLAZE
  1 **cup confectioners' sugar**
  ½ **tsp. vanilla extract**
  1 **to 2 Tbsp. 2% milk**

1. In a large bowl, dissolve yeast in warm milk. Add the pumpkin, sugar, butter, salt and 4¾ cups flour. Beat until smooth. Stir in enough of the remaining flour to form a soft dough (dough will be sticky).

2. Turn the dough onto a floured surface; knead until smooth and elastic, 6-8 minutes. Place in a greased bowl, turning once to grease top. Cover and let rise in a warm place until doubled, about 1 hour.

3. Punch dough down; divide in half. Roll each portion into a 12x10-in. rectangle. Combine the flour, brown sugar, cinnamon and allspice; cut in butter until crumbly. Set aside 1 cup.

4. Sprinkle remaining streusel over dough to within ½ in. of edges; press down lightly. Roll up jelly-roll style, starting with a long side; pinch seams to seal.

5. Cut each roll into 12 slices. Place cut side down in two greased 13x9-in. baking pans. Sprinkle with reserved streusel. Cover pans and let dough rise until doubled, about 30 minutes.

6. Bake at 375° for 20-25 minutes or until golden brown. Meanwhile, combine the confectioners' sugar, vanilla and enough milk to achieve desired consistency. Drizzle over rolls. Serve warm.

1 ROLL: 285 cal., 10g fat (6g sat. fat), 26mg chol., 176mg sod., 45g carb. (19g sugars, 1g fiber), 4g pro.

SNACKS, DIPS & SIPS

PUMPKIN SPICE LATTE

TAKES: 20 MIN. • **MAKES:** 6 SERVINGS

- 3 cups 2% milk
- ¾ cup canned pumpkin
- ⅓ cup packed brown sugar
- ½ tsp. ground cinnamon
- ¼ tsp. ground ginger
- ⅛ tsp. ground nutmeg
- 1½ cups hot brewed espresso or strong-brewed dark roast coffee
  Whipped cream and additional nutmeg, optional

Place first six ingredients in a large saucepan. Cook and stir over medium heat until heated through. Stir in hot espresso. Pour into warm mugs. Top with whipped cream and additional nutmeg if desired.

1 SERVING: 124 cal., 3g fat (2g sat. fat), 10mg chol., 71mg sod., 22g carb. (19g sugars, 1g fiber), 4g pro.

"Every sip of this spiced-right beverage tastes just like a yummy piece of pumpkin pie with whipped cream!"
—TASTE OF HOME TEST KITCHEN

NOTES

FESTIVE PUMPKIN DIP

You can either serve this snack dip in bread, per the recipe, or you can dress it up by serving it in a festive pumpkin.

—EVELYN KENNELL, ROANOKE, IL

PREP: 20 MIN. + CHILLING • **MAKES:** 3 CUPS

- 12 oz. cream cheese, softened
- ¾ cup canned pumpkin
- 2 Tbsp. taco seasoning
- ⅛ tsp. garlic powder
- ⅓ cup chopped dried beef
- ⅓ cup chopped green pepper
- ⅓ cup chopped sweet red pepper
- 1 can (2¼ oz.) sliced ripe olives, drained
- 1 round loaf (1 lb.) Italian or pumpernickel bread, optional
  Fresh vegetables, crackers or corn chips

1. In a bowl, beat cream cheese, pumpkin, taco seasoning and garlic powder until smooth. Stir in beef, peppers and olives. Cover and refrigerate until serving.

2. If desired, just before serving, cut top off of bread; scoop bread from inside, leaving a ½-in. shell (save the bread from inside to make croutons or bread crumbs or save for another use). Fill shell with cream cheese mixture. Serve with vegetables, crackers or corn chips.

2 TBSP.: 112 cal., 6g fat (3g sat. fat), 15mg chol., 264mg sod., 12g carb. (2g sugars, 1g fiber), 3g pro.

HELPFUL HINT

Little jars or cans of dried beef, also known as chipped beef, were once an American staple. They don't require refrigeration before opening. You can substitute finely chopped deli roast beef if desired.

ROASTED FRESH PUMPKIN SEEDS

I learned how to roast pumpkin seeds from my mother, who learned it from her mother. It's a wholesome, healthy snack and fun to make after you finish carving the Halloween jack-o'-lantern.

—MARGARET DRYE, PLAINFIELD, NH

PREP: 20 MIN. + SOAKING
BAKE: 1½ HOURS + COOLING
MAKES: 1½ CUPS

- 2 cups fresh pumpkin seeds
- 1 tsp. salt
- 1 Tbsp. olive oil
- ¾ tsp. kosher or fine sea salt

1. Place pumpkin seeds in a 1-qt. bowl; cover with water. Stir in salt; let stand, covered, overnight.
2. Preheat oven to 200°. Drain and rinse seeds; drain again and pat dry. Transfer to a 15x10x1-in. baking pan. Toss with oil and kosher salt; spread in a single layer.
3. Roast 1½-1¾ hours or until crisp and lightly browned, stirring occasionally. Cool completely. Store seeds in an airtight container.

¼ CUP: 115 cal., 6g fat (1g sat. fat), 0 chol., 248mg sod., 11g carb. (0 sugars, 4g fiber), 4g pro. DIABETIC EXCHANGES: 1 fat, ½ starch.

JACK-O'-LANTERN EMPANADAS

Your Halloween party crowd will love these spooktacular pockets with silly grins. The savory filling is perfectly spiced, and refrigerated pastry makes prep easy.

—MATTHEW HASS, FRANKLIN, WI

PREP: 45 MIN. • **BAKE:** 15 MIN.
MAKES: 2½ DOZEN

- 1 Tbsp. canola oil
- ½ cup frozen corn
- ¼ cup finely chopped onion
- ¼ cup finely chopped sweet red pepper
- 2 garlic cloves, minced
- 1 can (15 oz.) solid-pack pumpkin
- ½ cup black beans, rinsed and drained
- 2 tsp. chili powder
- ¾ tsp. salt
- ¾ tsp. ground cumin
- ½ tsp. dried oregano
- 2 pkg. (14.1 oz. each) refrigerated pie pastry
- 1 large egg
- 1 Tbsp. water

1. Preheat oven to 425°. In a large skillet, heat oil over medium heat. Add corn, onion and pepper; cook and stir 2-3 minutes or until tender. Add minced garlic; cook 1 minute longer. Stir in pumpkin, black beans and seasonings; heat through. Cool mixture slightly.

2. On a lightly floured surface, unroll pastry sheets. With a 3-in. floured pumpkin-shaped or round cookie cutter, cut 60 pumpkins, rerolling dough as necessary. Place half of the pumpkins 2 in. apart on parchment paper-lined baking sheets; top each with about 1 Tbsp. pumpkin mixture. Using a knife, cut jack-o'-lantern faces or slits in the remaining pastries. Place over the top of the pumpkin mixture; press edges with a fork to seal.

3. In a small bowl, whisk egg and water; brush over the pastries. Bake until golden brown, 12-15 minutes. Remove from pans to wire racks .

1 EMPANADA: 137 cal., 8g fat (3g sat. fat), 11mg chol., 174mg sod., 15g carb. (2g sugars, 1g fiber), 2g pro.

SPICED PUMPKIN COFFEE SHAKES

The winter holidays are my favorite time of year, and this spiced pumpkin drink is one reason I love the season so much. If you don't have a coffee maker, it's okay to use instant coffee in this recipe.

—KATHIE PEREZ, EAST PEORIA, IL

PREP: 15 MIN. + CHILLING • **MAKES:** 6 SERVINGS

- 2 **cups whole milk**
- ½ **cup canned pumpkin**
- 2 **Tbsp. sugar**
- 1 **tsp. pumpkin pie spice**
- 1 **cup strong brewed coffee**
- 3 **tsp. vanilla extract**
- 4 **cups vanilla ice cream**
- 1 **cup crushed ice**
  Sweetened whipped cream and additional pumpkin pie spice

1. In a small saucepan, heat the milk, pumpkin, sugar and pie spice until bubbles form around sides of pan and sugar is dissolved. Transfer to a bowl; stir in coffee and vanilla. Refrigerate, covered, several hours or overnight.

2. Place milk mixture, ice cream and ice in a blender; cover and process until blended. Serve immediately with whipped cream; sprinkle with additional pie spice.

1 SERVING: 262 cal., 12g fat (8g sat. fat), 47mg chol., 107mg sod., 31g carb. (28g sugars, 1g fiber), 6g pro.

ROASTED PUMPKIN NACHOS

In the summer, I made this dish with black beans and corn off the cob. Wanting to try it with fall ingredients, I replaced the corn with roasted pumpkin—yum! It's also good with butternut squash.

—LESLE HARWOOD, DOUGLASSVILLE, PA

PREP: 40 MIN. • **BAKE:** 10 MIN.
MAKES: 12 SERVINGS

- 4 cups cubed fresh pumpkin or butternut squash (about 1 lb.)
- 2 Tbsp. olive oil
- ¼ tsp. salt
- ⅛ tsp. pepper
- 1 pkg. (13 oz.) tortilla chips
- 1 can (15 oz.) black beans, rinsed and drained
- 1 jar (16 oz.) salsa
- 3 cups shredded Mexican cheese blend
  Optional toppings: minced fresh cilantro, sliced green onions and hot pepper sauce

1. Preheat oven to 400°. Place pumpkin in a greased 15x10x1-in. baking pan. Drizzle with oil; sprinkle with salt and pepper. Toss to coat. Roast 25-30 minutes or until tender, stirring occasionally.

2. Reduce the oven setting to 350°. On a greased 15x10x1-in. baking pan, layer half each of the chips, beans, pumpkin, salsa and cheese. Repeat layers. Bake 8-10 minutes or until cheese is melted. Add toppings of your choice; serve immediately.

1 SERVING: 347 cal., 18g fat (6g sat. fat), 25mg chol., 559mg sod., 36g carb. (3g sugars, 4g fiber), 10g pro.

HELPFUL HINT

To turn this vegetarian appetizer into a meat lover's dream, top it with some crumbled cooked chorizo or taco meat.

PUMPKIN PIE DIP

TAKES: 10 MIN. • **MAKES:** 4 CUPS

- 1 pkg. (8 oz.) cream cheese, softened
- 2 cups confectioners' sugar
- 1 cup canned pumpkin
- ½ cup sour cream
- 1 tsp. ground cinnamon
- 1 tsp. pumpkin pie spice
- ½ tsp. ground ginger
  Gingersnap cookies

Beat cream cheese and confectioners' sugar until smooth. Beat in pumpkin, sour cream and spices until blended. Transfer to a bowl; serve with gingersnaps. Refrigerate leftovers.

2 TBSP.: 65 cal., 3g fat (2g sat. fat), 8mg chol., 24mg sod., 9g carb. (8g sugars, 0 fiber), 1g pro.

I came up with this rich, creamy dip when I had a small amount of canned pumpkin left in the fridge after my holiday baking. It's also great served with sliced pears and apples or as a spread on zucchini bread or any nut bread.

—LAURIE LaCLAIR, NORTH RICHLAND HILLS, TX

PUMPKIN SPICE HOT CHOCOLATE

My mom makes this hot chocolate with pumpkin, spices and white chocolate. We usually drink it on Halloween, but it's delish at Christmas, too.

—SASHA KING, WESTLAKE VILLAGE, CA

TAKES: 30 MIN. • **MAKES:** 14 SERVINGS

- 1 cup heavy whipping cream
- 3 Tbsp. sugar
- 3 tsp. vanilla extract

HOT CHOCOLATE

- 8 cups 2% milk
- 4 cups heavy whipping cream
- 2 cinnamon sticks (3 in.)
- 2 Tbsp. pumpkin pie spice
- 1 Tbsp. grated orange zest
- 1 can (15 oz.) solid-pack pumpkin
- 1 cup sugar
- 1 cup white baking chips
- 1 Tbsp. vanilla extract
  Additional pumpkin pie spice

1. In a medium bowl, beat cream until it begins to thicken. Add sugar and vanilla; beat until stiff peaks form. Refrigerate until serving.

2. In a 6-qt. stockpot, heat milk, cream, cinnamon sticks, pie spice and orange zest over medium heat until bubbles form around sides of pan.

3. Whisk pumpkin, sugar and baking chips into the milk mixture until blended. Remove from heat; stir in vanilla. Discard cinnamon sticks. Pour into mugs; top with whipped cream. Sprinkle with additional pie spice. Serve immediately.

1 SERVING: 511 cal., 38g fat (24g sat. fat), 111mg chol., 102mg sod., 37g carb. (35g sugars, 1g fiber), 8g pro.

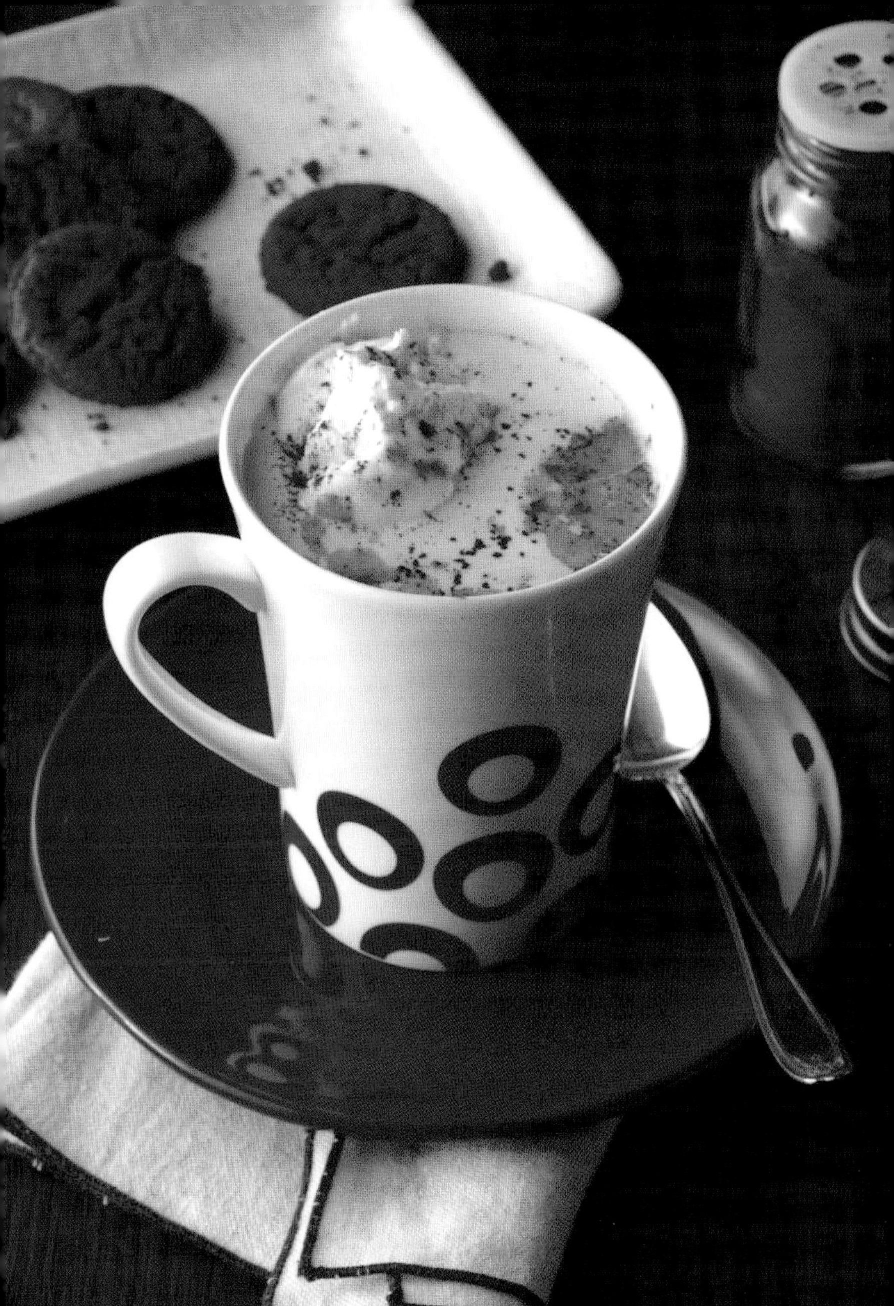

PUMPKIN PINWHEELS

Cream cheese, mozzarella and roasted red peppers make these spirited pinwheels devilishly delicious. They were a hit at my last Halloween party.

—ANNDREA BAILEY, HUNTINGTON BEACH, CA

PREP: 15 MIN. + CHILLING • **BAKE:** 20 MIN. • **MAKES:** 32 PINWHEELS

- 2 pkg. (8 oz. each) cream cheese, softened
- 1 cup shredded part-skim mozzarella cheese
- ½ cup chopped roasted sweet red peppers, drained
- ¼ tsp. Italian seasoning
- ¼ tsp. garlic salt
- ¼ tsp. onion powder
- 2 tubes (8 oz. each) refrigerated crescent rolls
  Pretzel sticks and fresh cilantro leaves, optional

1. Preheat oven to 350°. Beat cream cheese until smooth. Beat in mozzarella, roasted red peppers and seasonings until blended. Unroll tubes of crescent dough and separate each into two rectangles; press perforations to seal.

2. Spread the cheese mixture over each rectangle. Roll up jelly-roll style, starting with a short side; pinch seam to seal. Wrap in plastic, and chill at least 1 hour.

3. Cut each roll crosswise into eight slices; place slices on ungreased baking sheets, cut side down. Bake until golden brown, 20-22 minutes. If desired, decorate with pretzel sticks and cilantro leaves to look like pumpkins.

1 PINWHEEL: 112 cal., 8g fat (3g sat. fat), 17mg chol., 204mg sod., 7g carb. (2g sugars, 0 fiber), 3g pro.

PUMPKIN PIE SHOTS

Set out a batch of these grown-up treats and get ready for the compliments. They can be prepared ahead of time, making them a great party starter.
—TASTE OF HOME TEST KITCHEN

PREP: 25 MIN. + CHILLNG
MAKES: 12 SERVINGS

- 1 envelope unflavored gelatin
- 1 cup cold water
- ⅓ cup canned pumpkin
- ¼ cup sugar
- ½ tsp. pumpkin pie spice
- ⅓ cup butterscotch schnapps liqueur
- ¼ cup vodka
- 1½ tsp. heavy whipping cream
  Sweetened whipped cream

1. In a small saucepan, sprinkle gelatin over cold water; let stand 1 minute. Heat and stir over low heat until the gelatin is completely dissolved. Stir in pumpkin, sugar and pie spice; cook and stir until sugar is dissolved. Remove from heat. Stir in liqueur, vodka and whipping cream.
2. Pour into twelve 2-oz. shot glasses; refrigerate until set. Top with sweetened whipped cream.

1 SERVING: 139 cal., 11g fat (7g sat. fat), 34mg chol., 10mg sod., 6g carb. (5g sugars, 0 fiber), 1g pro.

PUMPKIN BUTTER

Biting into this spiced butter on a hot biscuit is absolutely heavenly. With a dash of whipped cream, you might think you were eating pumpkin pie!

—JUNE BARRUS, SPRINGVILLE, UT

PREP: 5 MIN. • COOK: 20 MIN. + COOLING • MAKES: 6 CUPS

- 3 cans (15 oz. each) solid-pack pumpkin
- 2 cups sugar
- 1½ cups water
- 3 Tbsp. lemon juice
- 1 Tbsp. grated lemon zest
- 3 tsp. ground cinnamon
- ¾ tsp. salt
- ¾ tsp. ground nutmeg
- ¾ tsp. ground ginger

1. In a large saucepan, combine all ingredients. Bring to a boil, stirring frequently. Reduce heat; cover and simmer for 20 minutes to allow flavors to blend.

2. Cool. Spoon into jars. Cover and store in the refrigerator for up to 3 weeks.

2 TBSP.: 42 cal., 0 fat (0 sat. fat), 0 chol., 38mg sod., 11g carb. (9g sugars, 1g fiber), 0 pro.

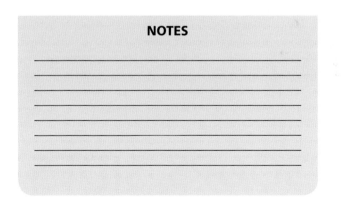

NOTES

_____

_____

_____

_____

_____

_____

_____

SOUPS, SIDES & MAIN DISHES

SAUSAGE & RICE STUFFED PUMPKINS

My children often request this dish, and it adds wow to any festive buffet table.

—ANDRIA PECKHAM, LOWELL, MI

PREP: 30 MIN. • **BAKE:** 55 MIN. • **MAKES:** 12 SERVINGS

   3 small pie pumpkins (about 2 lbs. each)
 ½ lb. bulk sweet Italian sausage
   1 lb. fresh mushrooms, chopped
   2 medium onions, chopped
   1 medium green pepper, chopped
   2 garlic cloves, minced
   4 cups cooked long grain rice
   1 cup grated Parmesan cheese, divided
   2 large eggs, lightly beaten
 ¼ cup minced fresh parsley
   1 tsp. salt
 ½ tsp. dried thyme

1. Preheat oven to 450°. Cut a 3-in. circle around each pumpkin stem. Remove tops and set aside. Remove strings and seeds from pumpkins; discard seeds or save for toasting.

2. In a large skillet, cook sausage, vegetables and garlic over medium heat 6-8 minutes or until sausage is no longer pink, breaking up sausage into crumbles; drain. Remove from the heat; stir in rice, ¾ cup cheese, eggs, parsley, salt and thyme.

3. Place pumpkins in a 15x10x1-in. baking pan and fill them with rice mixture. Replace pumpkin tops. Bake 30 minutes.

4. Reduce oven setting to 350°. Bake 25-35 minutes longer or until pumpkin is tender when pierced with a knife and a thermometer inserted in the filling reads 160°. Sprinkle remaining cheese over filling. Cut to serve.

¼ **PUMPKIN WITH** ⅔ **CUP FILLING:** 204 cal., 6g fat (2g sat. fat), 49mg chol., 405mg sod., 30g carb. (5g sugars, 2g fiber), 10g pro. **DIABETIC EXCHANGES:** 2 starch, 1 high-fat meat.

PUMPKIN GOAT CHEESE PASTA ALFREDO WITH BACON

This is a unique and delicious pasta, perfect for fall. I made it for my girlfriends and everyone asked for the recipe!

—ASHLEY LECKER, GREEN BAY, WI

PREP: 35 MIN. • **BAKE:** 20 MIN. • **MAKES:** 10 SERVINGS

- 1 package (16 ounces) cellentani or spiral pasta
- 4 Tbsp. butter
- 1 Tbsp. olive oil
- 3 garlic cloves, minced
- 2 shallots, minced
- 2 cups heavy whipping cream
- 1 cup whole milk
- 4 oz. crumbled goat cheese
- ½ cup grated Parmesan cheese
- ½ cup canned pumpkin
- ½ tsp. white pepper
- 2 Tbsp. chopped fresh sage

TOPPINGS

- 1 lb. bacon strips, cooked and crumbled
- 2 oz. crumbled goat cheese
- ¼ cup grated Parmesan cheese

1. Preheat the oven to 350°. Cook cellentani according to package instructions.

2. Meanwhile, in a large saucepan, heat butter and olive oil over medium heat. Add the garlic and shallots; cook and stir 1-2 minutes. Add the next six ingredients. Reduce heat to low. Cook, stirring constantly, until reduced, 6-8 minutes. Add sage. Remove from heat.

3. Drain pasta; gently stir into cream sauce. Transfer to a greased 13x9-in. baking dish. Top with bacon, goat cheese and Parmesan. Bake, covered, for 15 minutes. Uncover pasta; bake until cheeses are melted, about 5 minutes longer.

1 CUP: 559 cal., 37g fat (20g sat. fat), 111mg chol., 535mg sod., 40g carb. (5g sugars, 3g fiber), 19g pro.

HELPFUL HINT

Medium-grind cornmeal is great for polenta; finely ground can result in a paste-like texture. For improved nutrition, use stone-ground or water-ground cornmeal, which has more bran and germ than large commercial types and up to 2½ times the fiber.

CREAMY PUMPKIN POLENTA

Sometimes I like to hollow out a pumpkin and serve this creamy, hearty polenta inside it. The crunchy pumpkin seeds add great texture.

—DEBI GEORGE, MANSFIELD, TX

....

TAKES: 25 MIN. • **MAKES:** 6 SERVINGS

5⅓ cups water
1 tsp. salt
1⅓ cups yellow cornmeal
½ tsp. ground nutmeg
¾ cup canned pumpkin
½ cup cream cheese, cubed
Salted pumpkin seeds or pepitas, optional

1. In a large heavy saucepan, bring water and salt to a boil.
2. Reduce heat to a gentle boil; slowly whisk in cornmeal and nutmeg. Cook and stir with a wooden spoon for 15-20 minutes or until the polenta is thickened and pulls away cleanly from the sides of the pan. Stir in pumpkin and cream cheese until smooth. Sprinkle each serving with pumpkin seeds if desired.

¾ **CUP:** 191 cal., 7g fat (4g sat. fat), 21mg chol., 453mg sod., 27g carb. (1g sugars, 4g fiber), 5g pro. **DIABETIC EXCHANGES:** 2 starch, 1 fat.

PUMPKIN-CHORIZO BOW TIES

Chicken sausage is such a convenient way to add flavor to healthy dishes. If your family doesn't like spicy food, skip the red pepper flakes and use a mild-flavored sausage.
—SHARON RICCI, MENDON, NY

TAKES: 25 MIN. • **MAKES:** 4 SERVINGS

- 3 cups uncooked multigrain bow tie pasta
- 1 tsp. canola oil
- 1 pkg. (12 oz.) fully cooked chorizo chicken sausage links or other spicy chicken sausage, cut into ¼-in. slices
- 1 cup fat-free half-and-half
- 1 cup canned pumpkin
- ½ cup shredded Mexican cheese blend
- ⅛ tsp. garlic powder
- ⅛ tsp. crushed red pepper flakes
- 1 Tbsp. minced fresh cilantro

1. Cook pasta according to package directions. Meanwhile, in a large skillet, heat oil over medium-high heat. Add chicken sausage; cook and stir for 4-6 minutes or until browned. Stir in half-and-half, pumpkin, cheese blend, garlic powder and pepper flakes; heat through.

2. Drain pasta. Add to sausage mixture; toss to coat. Sprinkle with cilantro.

1¼ CUPS: 506 cal., 15g fat (5g sat. fat), 78mg chol., 732mg sod., 60g carb. (11g sugars, 6g fiber), 32g pro.

PUMPKIN SEED BAKED CHICKEN

For a fun coating on baked chicken, I use pumpkin seeds and cheese crackers to make it crunchy on the outside and super tender on the inside.

—NANCY HEISHMAN, LAS VEGAS, NV

PREP: 20 MIN. • **BAKE:** 30 MIN.
MAKES: 4 SERVINGS

- ½ cup finely crushed cheese crackers (about 1 cup whole)
- 2 tsp. paprika
- ½ tsp. salt
- ½ tsp. garlic powder
- ¼ tsp. pepper
- ⅔ cup salted pumpkin seeds or pepitas, divided
- 1 large egg
- 3 Tbsp. honey
- 2 Tbsp. lemon juice
- 4 boneless skinless chicken breast halves (6 oz. each)

1. Preheat oven to 350°. Place first five ingredients and 3 Tbsp. of the pumpkin seeds in a shallow bowl. Finely chop remaining pumpkin seeds; stir into cracker mixture. In another shallow bowl, whisk together egg, honey and lemon juice. Dip both sides of chicken in egg mixture, then in crumb mixture, patting to adhere.

2. Bake on a greased baking sheet until a thermometer reads 165°, 30-35 minutes.

1 CHICKEN BREAST HALF : 378 cal., 16g fat (4g sat. fat), 118mg chol., 525mg sod., 16g carb. (7g sugars, 2g fiber), 42g pro.

BLACK BEAN & PUMPKIN CHILI

My family is crazy about this slow cooker chili because it uses ingredients you don't usually find in chili. Believe it or not, pumpkin is what makes this dish so special. Cook up a big batch and freeze some for later; it tastes even better reheated.

—DEBORAH VLIET, HOLLAND, MI

PREP: 20 MIN. • **COOK:** 4 HOURS • **MAKES:** 10 SERVINGS

- 2 Tbsp. olive oil
- 1 medium onion, chopped
- 1 medium sweet yellow pepper, chopped
- 3 garlic cloves, minced
- 2 cans (15 oz. each) black beans, rinsed and drained
- 1 can (15 oz.) solid-pack pumpkin
- 1 can (14½ oz.) diced tomatoes, undrained
- 3 cups chicken broth
- 2½ cups cubed cooked turkey
- 2 tsp. dried parsley flakes
- 2 tsp. chili powder
- 1½ tsp. ground cumin
- 1½ tsp. dried oregano
- ½ tsp. salt
  Cubed avocado and thinly sliced green onions, optional

1. In a large skillet, heat oil over medium-high heat. Add onion and pepper; cook and stir until tender. Add garlic; cook 1 minute longer.

2. Transfer mixture to a 5-qt. slow cooker; stir in the next 10 ingredients. Cook, covered, on low 4-5 hours. If desired, top with avocado and green onions.

1 CUP: 192 cal., 5g fat (1g sat. fat), 28mg chol., 658mg sod., 21g carb. (5g sugars, 7g fiber), 16g pro. **DIABETIC EXCHANGES:** 2 lean meat, 1½ starch, ½ fat.

HELPFUL HINT

This soup is satisfying and good for you. To make it even healthier, sub in reduced-sodium chicken broth for regular. This simple swap reduces the sodium to just 535mg per cup.

TURKEY MASHED POTATO CHIMIS

Bet you've never had a chimichanga quite like this! A homemade sauce of pumpkin puree and chipotle peppers gives these delicious chimis a spicy-sweet finish.

—SHERRI GORDON, OLMSTED FALLS, OH

PREP: 30 MIN. • **BAKE:** 35 MIN. • **MAKES:** 12 SERVINGS

- 4 medium potatoes, peeled and cut into ½-in. cubes
- ¼ cup butter, cubed
- ¼ cup half-and-half cream
- ¼ tsp. salt
- ⅛ tsp. pepper
- 4 cups cubed cooked turkey breast
- 2 cups shredded Monterey Jack cheese
- 12 flour tortillas (8 in.), warmed
- 5 Tbsp. butter, melted

CHIPOTLE PUMPKIN SAUCE

- 1 cup canned pumpkin
- 1 tsp. minced chipotle pepper in adobo sauce
- 1 cup salsa
- ½ cup shredded Parmesan cheese
- ½ cup heavy whipping cream

1. Place potatoes in a large saucepan and cover with water. Bring to a boil. Reduce heat; cover and cook 10-15 minutes or until tender. Drain.

2. Mash potatoes with butter, cream, salt and pepper. Stir in turkey and cheese.

3. Brush tortillas with melted butter. Place ⅔ cup potato mixture down the center of each tortilla. Fold sides and ends over filling and roll up. Place seam side down in two greased 13x9-in. baking dishes. Brush with leftover melted butter.

4. Bake, uncovered, at 375° for 35-40 minutes or until edges are lightly browned.

5. In a small saucepan, combine the sauce ingredients; heat through (do not boil). Drizzle over chimichangas.

1 SERVING: 467 cal., 23g fat (13g sat. fat), 98mg chol., 629mg sod., 38g carb. (2g sugars, 2g fiber), 26g pro.

PUMPKIN GNOCCHI IN SAGE BUTTER

For a delicious autumn spin on an Italian classic, try this hearty seasonal gnocchi. Sage and garlic butter complement the pumpkin wonderfully.

—DONNA MOSCA KAHLER, JUPITER, FL

PREP: 30 MIN. • **COOK:** 5 MIN. • **MAKES:** 4 SERVINGS

- 1½ cups all-purpose flour
- ¼ tsp. salt
- ¼ tsp. pepper
- ⅛ tsp. ground nutmeg
- 1 cup canned pumpkin
- 6 qt. water
- ½ cup butter, cubed
- 4 fresh sage leaves, thinly sliced
- 1 garlic clove, minced

1. In a small bowl, combine the flour, salt, pepper and nutmeg. Stir in pumpkin until blended. On a lightly floured surface, knead 10-12 times, forming a soft dough. Let rest for 10 minutes.

2. Divide dough into four portions. On a lightly floured surface, roll each portion into a ½-in.-thick rope; cut into ¾-in. pieces. Press and roll each piece with a lightly floured fork.

3. In a Dutch oven, bring water to a boil. Cook gnocchi in batches for 1-1½ minutes or until they float. Remove with a slotted spoon; keep warm.

4. In a large heavy saucepan, melt butter over medium heat. Add the sage, garlic and gnocchi; stir to coat.

⅔ **CUP:** 394 cal., 23g fat (14g sat. fat), 60mg chol., 312mg sod., 41g carb. (3g sugars, 4g fiber), 6g pro.

ROASTED PUMPKIN & BRUSSELS SPROUTS

PREP: 15 MIN. • **BAKE:** 35 MIN.
MAKES: 8 SERVINGS

- 1 medium pie pumpkin (about 3 lbs.), peeled and cut into ¾-in. cubes
- 1 lb. fresh Brussels sprouts, halved lengthwise
- 4 garlic cloves, thinly sliced
- ⅓ cup olive oil
- 2 Tbsp. balsamic vinegar
- 1 tsp. sea salt
- ½ tsp. coarsely ground pepper
- 2 Tbsp. minced fresh parsley

1. Preheat oven to 400°. In a large bowl, combine pumpkin, Brussels sprouts and garlic. Whisk oil, vinegar, salt and pepper; drizzle over vegetables and toss to coat.
2. Transfer to a greased 15x10x1-in. baking pan. Roast 35-40 minutes or until tender, stirring once. Sprinkle with parsley.

¾ **CUP:** 152 cal., 9g fat (1g sat. fat), 0 chol., 255mg sod., 17g carb. (4g sugars, 3g fiber), 4g pro. **DIABETIC EXCHANGES:** 2 fat, 1 starch.

"While traveling to Taiwan, we visited a restaurant where fresh vegetables including pumpkin were served. That inspired me to roast pumpkin with Brussels sprouts for special occasions. "

—**PAM CORRELL, BROCKPORT, PA**

PUMPKIN HARVEST BEEF STEW

By the time the stew is done simmering and a batch of bread finishes baking, the house smells absolutely wonderful.

—MARCIA O'NEIL, CEDAR CREST, NM

PREP: 25 MIN. • **COOK:** 6½ HOURS • **MAKES:** 6 SERVINGS

- 1 Tbsp. canola oil
- 1 beef top round steak (1½ lbs.), cut into 1-in. cubes
- 1½ cups cubed peeled pie pumpkin or sweet potatoes
- 3 small red potatoes, peeled and cubed
- 1 cup cubed acorn squash
- 1 medium onion, chopped
- 2 cans (14½ oz. each) reduced-sodium beef broth
- 1 can (14½ oz.) diced tomatoes, undrained
- 2 bay leaves
- 2 garlic cloves, minced
- 2 tsp. reduced-sodium beef bouillon granules
- ½ tsp. chili powder
- ½ tsp. pepper
- ¼ tsp. ground allspice
- ¼ tsp. ground cloves
- ¼ cup water
- 3 Tbsp. all-purpose flour

1. In a large skillet, heat oil over medium-high heat. Brown beef in batches; remove with a slotted spoon to a 4- or 5-qt. slow cooker. Add the pumpkin, potatoes, squash and onion. Stir in the broth, tomatoes and seasonings. Cover and cook on low for 6-8 hours or until meat is tender.

2. Remove bay leaves. In a small bowl, mix water and flour until smooth; gradually stir into stew. Cover and cook on high for 30 minutes or until liquid is thickened.

1⅔ CUPS: 258 cal., 6g fat (1g sat. fat), 67mg chol., 479mg sod., 21g carb. (6g sugars, 4g fiber), 29g pro. **DIABETIC EXCHANGES:** 3 lean meat, 1 starch, 1 vegetable, ½ fat.

PUMPKIN LASAGNA

Even friends who aren't big fans of pumpkin are surprised by this delectable lasagna. Canned pumpkin and no-cook noodles make it a cinch to prepare.

—TAMARA HURON, NEW MARKET, AL

PREP: 25 MIN.
BAKE: 55 MIN. + STANDING
MAKES: 6 SERVINGS

- ½ lb. sliced fresh mushrooms
- 1 small onion, chopped
- ½ tsp. salt, divided
- 2 tsp. olive oil
- 1 can (15 oz.) solid-pack pumpkin
- ½ cup half-and-half cream
- 1 tsp. dried sage leaves
  Dash pepper
- 9 no-cook lasagna noodles
- 1 cup reduced-fat ricotta cheese
- 1 cup shredded part-skim mozzarella cheese
- ¾ cup shredded Parmesan cheese, divided

1. In a small skillet, saute the mushrooms, onion and ¼ tsp. salt in oil until tender; set aside. In a small bowl, combine the pumpkin, cream, sage, pepper and remaining salt.

2. Spread ½ cup pumpkin sauce in an 11x7-in. baking dish coated with cooking spray. Top with three noodles (the noodles will overlap slightly). Spread ½ cup pumpkin sauce to edges of noodles. Top with half of mushroom mixture, ½ cup ricotta, ½ cup mozzarella and ¼ cup Parmesan cheese. Repeat layers. Top with remaining noodles and sauce.

3. Cover; bake at 375° for 45 minutes. Uncover; sprinkle with remaining Parmesan cheese. Bake 10-15 minutes longer or until cheese is melted. Let stand for 10 minutes before cutting.

FREEZE OPTION Cover and freeze unbaked lasagna. To use, partially thaw in refrigerator overnight. Remove from the refrigerator 30 minutes before baking. Preheat the oven to 375°. Bake as directed, increasing time as necessary for a thermometer inserted in center to read 165°.

1 SERVING: 310 cal., 12g fat (6g sat. fat), 36mg chol., 497mg sod., 32g carb. (7g sugars, 5g fiber), 17g pro. **DIABETIC EXCHANGES:** 2 starch, 2 fat, 1 lean meat.

PUMPKIN-CURRY CHICKEN OVER CASHEW RICE

This is truly a dish that combines international flavors with homespun comfort. The sweet curry aroma alone will warm hearts on gray-sky days.
—AYSHA SCHURMAN, AMMON, ID

TAKES: 30 MIN. • **MAKES:** 5 SERVINGS

- 2 cups uncooked jasmine rice
- 1½ lbs. boneless skinless chicken breasts, cut into ½-in. cubes
- 4 tsp. curry powder, divided
- ¼ tsp. pepper
- 2 Tbsp. olive oil
- 1 garlic clove, minced
- 1 cup canned pumpkin
- ½ cup chicken broth
- ½ cup raisins
- ¼ cup apple butter
- ½ tsp. Chinese five-spice powder
- ⅓ cup chopped cashews, toasted
  Minced fresh parsley

1. Cook rice according to package directions.
2. Meanwhile, sprinkle chicken with 1 tsp. curry powder and pepper. In a large skillet, saute chicken in oil for 5-6 minutes or until no longer pink. Add garlic; cook 1 minute longer.
3. Stir in the pumpkin, broth, raisins, apple butter, five-spice powder and remaining curry powder. Bring to a boil. Reduce heat; simmer, uncovered, for 5-7 minutes to allow flavors to blend.
4. Stir cashews into cooked rice and serve with chicken mixture. Sprinkle with parsley.
NOTE This recipe was tested with commercially prepared apple butter.

1 CUP CHICKEN MIXTURE WITH 1 CUP RICE: 609 cal., 14g fat (3g sat. fat), 76mg chol., 232mg sod., 85g carb. (16g sugars, 5g fiber), 36g pro.

LENTIL PUMPKIN SOUP

PREP: 15 MIN. • **COOK:** 7 HOURS
MAKES: 6 SERVINGS

- 1 lb. red potatoes (about 4 medium), cut into 1-in. pieces
- 1 can (15 oz.) solid-pack pumpkin
- 1 cup dried lentils, rinsed
- 1 medium onion, chopped
- 3 garlic cloves, minced
- ½ tsp. ground ginger
- ½ tsp. pepper
- ⅛ tsp. salt
- 2 cans (14½ oz. each) vegetable broth
- 1½ cups water

In a 3-or 4-qt. slow cooker, combine all ingredients. Cook, covered, on low for 7-9 hours or until potatoes and lentils are tender.

1⅓ CUPS: 210 cal., 1g fat (0 sat. fat), 0 chol., 463mg sod., 42g carb. (5g sugars, 7g fiber), 11g pro. **DIABETIC EXCHANGES:** 3 starch, 1 lean meat.

"Garlic and spices brighten up my hearty pumpkin soup. It's just the thing we need on a chilly fall day. "

—LAURA MAGEE, HOULTON, WI

PASTA SQUIGGLES WITH PUMPKIN SAUCE

We love this fun change-of-pace pasta shape, particularly when it's dressed in a tasty pumpkin sauce. What a lovely addition to fall menus!
—LILY JULOW, LAWRENCEVILLE, GA

TAKES: 30 MIN. • **MAKES:** 6 SERVINGS

- **1** pkg. (16 oz.) cellentani or spiral pasta
- **2** Tbsp. butter
- **1** large onion, finely chopped
- **1** large sweet red pepper, finely chopped
- **3** garlic cloves, minced
- **2** cups chicken or vegetable broth
- **1** cup canned pumpkin
- **¼** cup heavy whipping cream
- **1** tsp. salt
- **¼** tsp. ground nutmeg
- **¼** tsp. pepper
- **¼** cup finely chopped fresh parsley
  Grated Parmesan cheese

1. In a Dutch oven, cook pasta according to package directions. In a large skillet, heat butter over medium heat. Add onion and red pepper; cook and stir 6-8 minutes or until tender. Add garlic; cook 1 minute longer. Stir in broth, pumpkin, cream, salt, nutmeg and pepper. Bring to a boil. Reduce heat; simmer, uncovered, 8-10 minutes or until slightly thickened.

2. Drain pasta and return to pan. Stir in pumpkin mixture and parsley. Sprinkle servings with cheese.

1½ CUPS: 381 cal., 10g fat (5g sat. fat), 26mg chol., 764mg sod., 64g carb. (7g sugars, 5g fiber), 12g pro.

SHREDDED BARBECUE CHICKEN OVER GRITS

There's nothing like juicy meat atop a pile of steaming grits. And the pumpkin in these grits makes them taste like a spicy, comforting bowl of fall flavors. Your family will come running to the table for this one.

—ERIN MYLROIE, SANTA CLARA, UT

PREP: 20 MIN. • **COOK:** 25 MIN.
MAKES: 6 SERVINGS

- 1 **lb. boneless skinless chicken breasts**
- ¼ **tsp. pepper**
- 1 **can (14½ oz.) reduced-sodium chicken broth, divided**
- 1 **cup hickory smoke-flavored barbecue sauce**
- ¼ **cup molasses**
- 1 **Tbsp. ground ancho chili pepper**
- ½ **tsp. ground cinnamon**
- 2¼ **cups water**
- 1 **cup quick-cooking grits**
- 1 **cup canned pumpkin**
- ¾ **cup shredded pepper jack cheese**
- 1 **medium tomato, seeded and chopped**
- 6 **Tbsp. reduced-fat sour cream**
- 2 **green onions, chopped**
- 2 **Tbsp. minced fresh cilantro**

1. Sprinkle chicken with pepper; place in a large nonstick skillet coated with cooking spray.

2. In a large bowl, combine 1 cup broth, barbecue sauce, molasses, chili pepper and cinnamon; pour over chicken. Bring to a boil. Reduce heat; cover and simmer for 20-25 minutes or until a thermometer reads 170°. Shred meat with two forks and return to the skillet.

3. Meanwhile, in a large saucepan, bring water and remaining broth to a boil. Slowly stir in the grits and pumpkin. Reduce heat; cook and stir 5-7 minutes or until thickened. Stir in cheese until melted.

4. Divide grits among six serving bowls; top each with ½ cup chicken mixture. Serve with tomato, sour cream, green onions and cilantro.

1 SERVING: 345 cal., 9g fat (4g sat. fat), 62mg chol., 718mg sod., 42g carb. (17g sugars, 4g fiber), 25g pro. **DIABETIC EXCHANGES:** 3 lean meat, 2½ starch, 1 fat.

POTATO PUMPKIN MASH

I swirl fresh pumpkin into potatoes for a little extra holiday color. No more plain white potatoes for us! If you'd like, you can substitute butternut squash for the pumpkin.

—MICHELLE MEDLEY, DALLAS, TX

PREP: 20 MIN. • **COOK:** 25 MIN. • **MAKES:** 8 SERVINGS

- 8 cups cubed peeled pie pumpkin (about 2 lbs.)
- 8 medium Yukon Gold potatoes, peeled and cubed (about 2 lbs.)
- ½ to ¾ cup 2% milk, divided
- 8 Tbsp. butter, softened, divided
- 1 tsp. salt, divided
- 1 Tbsp. olive oil
- ¼ tsp. coarsely ground pepper

1. Place pumpkin in a large saucepan; add water to cover. Bring to a boil. Reduce heat; cook, uncovered, for 20-25 minutes or until tender.

2. Meanwhile, place the potatoes in another saucepan; add water to cover. Bring to a boil. Reduce heat; cook, uncovered, for 10-15 minutes or until tender.

3. Drain potatoes; return to pan. Mash potatoes, adding ¼ cup milk, 4 Tbsp. butter and ½ tsp. salt. Add more milk if necessary to reach the desired consistency. Transfer to a serving bowl; keep warm.

4. Drain pumpkin; return to pan. Mash pumpkin, gradually adding the remaining butter and salt and enough remaining milk to reach desired consistency; spoon evenly over potatoes. Cut through mashed vegetables with a spoon or knife to swirl. Drizzle with olive oil; sprinkle with pepper. Serve immediately.

¾ **CUP:** 214 cal., 13 g fat (8 g sat. fat), 31 mg chol., 384 mg sod., 23 g carb., 2 g fiber, 3 g pro.

PIES, CAKES & CHEESECAKES

SOUR CREAM PUMPKIN CHEESECAKE

On the farm when I was young, we produced several ingredients for this longtime favorite. We raised pumpkins in our vegetable garden and made homemade butter and sour cream from our dairy herd.

—EVONNE WURMNEST, NORMAL, IL

PREP: 20 MIN. + CHILLING
BAKE: 55 MIN. + COOLING
MAKES: 16 SERVINGS

CRUST
- 1 cup graham cracker crumbs
- 1 Tbsp. sugar
- ¼ cup butter, melted

FILLING
- 2 pkg. (8 oz. each) cream cheese, softened
- ¾ cup sugar
- 2 large eggs
- 1 can (15 oz.) solid-pack pumpkin
- 1¼ tsp. ground cinnamon
- ½ tsp. ground ginger
- ½ tsp. ground nutmeg
- ¼ tsp. salt

TOPPING
- 2 cups sour cream
- 2 Tbsp. sugar
- 1 tsp. vanilla extract
- 12 to 16 pecan halves, chopped

1. In a small bowl, combine the graham cracker crumbs and sugar; stir in butter. Press into the bottom of a 9-in. springform pan; chill.

2. For the filling, in a large bowl, beat cream cheese and sugar until smooth. Add eggs, beat on low speed just until combined. Stir in the pumpkin, spices and salt.

3. Pour into crust. Place the pan on a baking sheet. Bake at 350° for 50 minutes.

4. Meanwhile, for topping, combine sour cream, sugar and vanilla until smooth. Spread over filling; return to the oven for 5 minutes. Cool on rack for 10 minutes. Carefully run a knife around the edge of pan to loosen; cool 1 hour longer.

5. Refrigerate overnight. Remove sides of pan. Top with chopped pecans. Refrigerate leftovers.

1 SLICE: 230 cal., 15g fat (9g sat. fat), 70mg chol., 164mg sod., 20g carb. (15g sugars, 2g fiber), 4g pro.

BUTTER PECAN PUMPKIN PIE

Whenever I serve this pie, everyone thinks I worked all day to make it, but it's actually easy to assemble. It's handy to have in the freezer when unexpected company stops in.

—ARLETTA SLOCUM, VENICE, FL

PREP: 20 MIN. + FREEZING • **MAKES:** 8 SERVINGS

- 1 qt. butter pecan ice cream, softened
- 1 pastry shell (9 in.), baked
- 1 cup canned pumpkin
- ½ cup sugar
- ¼ tsp. each ground cinnamon, ginger and nutmeg
- 1 cup heavy whipping cream, whipped
- ½ cup caramel ice cream topping
- ½ cup chocolate ice cream topping, optional
  Additional whipped cream

1. Spread ice cream into the crust; freeze for 2 hours or until firm.

2. In a small bowl, combine the pumpkin, sugar, cinnamon, ginger and nutmeg; fold in whipped cream. Spread over ice cream. Cover and freeze for 2 hours or until firm. May be frozen for up to 2 months.

3. Remove from the freezer 15 minutes before slicing. Drizzle with caramel ice cream topping. Drizzle with chocolate ice cream topping if desired. Dollop with whipped cream.

1 SLICE: 452 cal., 25g fat (11g sat. fat), 51mg chol., 289mg sod., 56g carb. (41g sugars, 1g fiber), 5g pro.

AUTUMN PUMPKIN CUPCAKES

These yummy pumpkin cupcakes are draped in cream cheese frosting and drizzled with a homemade salted caramel sauce. They're sweet and so tasty.

—WENDY RUSCH, CAMERON, WI

PREP: 30 MIN. • **BAKE:** 20 MIN. + COOLING
MAKES: 2 DOZEN

- 2 **cups sugar**
- 1 **can (15 oz.) solid-pack pumpkin**
- 4 **large eggs**
- ¾ **cup canola oil**
- 1 **tsp. vanilla extract**
- 2 **cups all-purpose flour**
- 2 **tsp. baking soda**
- 2 **tsp. pumpkin pie spice**
- 1 **tsp. salt**
- 1 **tsp. baking powder**

SAUCE
- ½ **cup packed brown sugar**
- 6 **Tbsp. heavy whipping cream**
- ¼ **cup butter, cubed**
- ⅛ **tsp. salt**
- ½ **tsp. vanilla extract**

FROSTING
- 1 **pkg. (8 oz.) cream cheese, softened**
- 1 **cup butter, softened**
- 1 **tsp. vanilla extract**
- 3 **cups confectioners' sugar**

1. Preheat the oven to 350°. Line 24 muffin cups with paper liners. In a large bowl, beat sugar, pumpkin, eggs, canola oil and vanilla until well blended. In another bowl, whisk flour, baking soda, pie spice, salt and baking powder; gradually beat into pumpkin mixture.

2. Fill prepared cups two-thirds full. Bake 20-22 minutes or until a toothpick inserted in center comes out clean. Cool in pans 10 minutes before removing to wire racks to cool completely.

3. For sauce, in a small heavy saucepan, combine brown sugar, cream, butter and salt; bring to a boil. Reduce heat; cook and stir 2-3 minutes or until thickened. Remove from heat; stir in vanilla. Cool to room temperature.

4. Meanwhile, in a large bowl, beat the cream cheese, butter and vanilla until blended. Gradually beat in the confectioners' sugar until smooth. Frost cupcakes; drizzle with sauce.

1 CUPCAKE: 391 cal., 22g fat (10g sat. fat), 70mg chol., 357mg sod., 47g carb. (37g sugars, 1g fiber), 3g pro.

RUM-GLAZED PUMPKIN CAKE

For years, my co-workers were taste testers as I worked on a recipe for pumpkin cake. This version wins, hands down.

—GILDA SMITH, SANTEE, CA

....

PREP: 20 MIN. • **BAKE:** 55 MIN. + COOLING
MAKES: 12 SERVINGS

- ½ **cup chopped pecans**
- 1 **can (15 oz.) solid-pack pumpkin**
- ½ **cup sugar**
- ½ **cup canola oil**
- 4 **large eggs**
- ¼ **cup water**
- 1 **pkg. yellow cake mix (regular size)**
- 1½ **tsp. ground cinnamon**
- ½ **tsp. ground nutmeg**
- ⅛ **tsp. ground cloves**

GLAZE

- 1 **cup sugar**
- ½ **cup butter, cubed**
- ¼ **tsp. ground cinnamon**
   Dash ground cloves
- ½ **cup rum**

1. Preheat oven to 350°. Grease and flour a 10-in. fluted tube pan; sprinkle pecans onto bottom of pan.

2. In a large bowl, beat the pumpkin, sugar, oil, eggs and water until well blended. In another bowl, whisk the cake mix and spices; gradually beat into pumpkin mixture. Transfer to prepared pan.

3. Bake 55-60 minutes or until a toothpick inserted in center comes out clean. Cool in pan 10 minutes before removing to a wire rack.

4. In a small saucepan, combine sugar, butter, cinnamon and cloves; cook and stir over medium heat until butter is melted. Remove from heat. Stir in rum; cook and stir 2-3 minutes longer or until sugar is dissolved.

5. Gradually brush glaze onto warm cake, about ¼ cup at a time, allowing glaze to soak into cake before adding more. Cool completely.

NOTE To remove cakes easily, use solid shortening to grease plain and fluted tube pans.

1 SLICE: 352 cal., 22g fat (7g sat. fat), 82mg chol., 113mg sod., 32g carb. (28g sugars, 2g fiber), 3g pro.

HELPFUL HINT

Pecans have a higher fat content than other nuts, so they're more prone to going rancid. They'll stay fresh for twice as long in the freezer as they would at room temperature.

WALNUT PUMPKIN CAKE ROLL

This is one of my family's favorite dessert recipes, especially for holiday gatherings.

—MARY GECHA, CENTER RUTLAND, VT

PREP: 20 MIN. + CHILLING
BAKE: 15 MIN. + COOLING
MAKES: 12 SERVINGS

- 3 large eggs
- 1 cup sugar
- ⅔ cup canned pumpkin
- 1 tsp. lemon juice
- ¾ cup all-purpose flour
- 2 tsp. ground cinnamon
- 1 tsp. baking powder
- 1 tsp. ground ginger
- ½ tsp. salt
- ½ tsp. ground nutmeg
- 1 cup finely chopped walnuts
  Confectioners' sugar

FILLING

- 6 oz. cream cheese, softened
- 1 cup confectioners' sugar
- ¼ cup butter, softened
- ½ tsp. vanilla extract

1. Line a greased 15x10x 1-in. baking pan with waxed paper. Grease the paper; set aside. In a bowl, beat eggs for 3 minutes. Gradually add sugar; beat for 2 minutes or until mixture becomes thick and lemon-colored. Stir in the pumpkin and lemon juice. Combine flour, cinnamon, baking powder, ginger, salt and nutmeg; fold into pumpkin mixture. Spread batter evenly in prepared pan. Sprinkle with the walnuts.

2. Bake at 375° for 12-14 minutes or until cake springs back when lightly touched in center. Cool for 5 minutes. Turn cake out of pan onto a kitchen towel dusted with confectioners' sugar. Gently peel off waxed paper. Roll up cake in towel jelly-roll style, starting with a long side. Cool completely on a wire rack.

3. In a bowl, beat filling ingredients until smooth. Unroll cake; spread evenly with filling to within ½ in. of edges. Roll up again without towel. Cover; refrigerate for 1 hour before cutting. Refrigerate leftovers.

1 SLICE: 312 cal., 17g fat (7g sat. fat), 81mg chol., 247mg sod., 36g carb. (26g sugars, 2g fiber), 6g pro.

WHITE CHOCOLATE PUMPKIN CHEESECAKE

Although my family enjoys all of the dishes I serve on Thanksgiving Day, it's this rich and creamy cheesecake they look forward to the most.
—**JOYCE SCHMIDT, LILBURN, GA**

PREP: 35 MIN. • **BAKE:** 50 MIN. + CHILLING
MAKES: 12 SERVINGS

- 1¼ **cups Oreo cookie crumbs**
- 2 **pkg. (8 oz. each) cream cheese, softened**
- ⅔ **cup sugar**
- 2 **tsp. vanilla extract**
- 3 **large eggs, lightly beaten**
- 8 **oz. white baking chocolate, melted and cooled**
- ½ **cup canned pumpkin**
- ¼ **tsp. each ground ginger, cinnamon and nutmeg**
  White chocolate curls and crushed Oreo cookies, optional

1. Place a greased 9-in. springform pan on a double thickness of heavy-duty foil (about 18 in. square). Wrap foil securely around pan.

2. Press cookie crumbs onto the bottom of prepared pan; set aside. In a large bowl, beat the cream cheese, sugar and vanilla until smooth. Add eggs; beat on low speed just until combined. Stir in melted chocolate.

3. In a small bowl, combine pumpkin and spices; gently fold into cream cheese mixture. Pour over crust. Place springform pan in a large baking pan; add 1 in. of hot water to larger pan.

4. Bake at 325° for 50-55 minutes or until center is almost set. Remove springform pan from water bath. Cool on a wire rack for 10 minutes. Carefully run a knife around edge of pan to loosen; cool 1 hour longer. Refrigerate overnight. Remove sides of pan; garnish with chocolate curls and crushed cookies if desired.

TEST KITCHEN TIPS

- It may be tempting to replace the white baking chocolate with white chocolate chips, but chips don't melt or blend as well as baking chocolate. Chocolate chips tend to seize (become granular) when folded into cheesecake batter.
- For beautiful chocolate curls, use a vegetable peeler and a big bar of chocolate. Room-temperature chocolate is more pliable, so make sure the chocolate you work with is not too cold!

1 PIECE: 369 cal., 23g fat (13g sat. fat), 85mg chol., 230mg sod., 37g carb. (31g sugars, 1g fiber), 6g pro.

CINNAMON PUMPKIN PIE

PREP: 10 MIN. • **BAKE:** 55 MIN. + COOLING • **MAKES:** 6 SERVINGS

- **1** cup sugar
- **4** tsp. cornstarch
- **½** tsp. salt
- **½** tsp. ground cinnamon
- **2** large eggs, lightly beaten
- **1** can (15 oz.) solid-pack pumpkin
- **1** cup whole milk
- **1** unbaked pastry shell (9 in.)
  Whipped cream in a can, optional

1. In a small bowl, combine the sugar, cornstarch, salt and cinnamon. In a large bowl, combine the eggs, pumpkin and sugar mixture. Gradually stir in milk. Pour into pastry shell.
2. Bake at 400° for 10 minutes. Reduce heat to 350°; bake 45-50 minutes longer or until a knife inserted in the center comes out clean. Cool on a wire rack. Top with whipped cream if desired. Refrigerate leftovers.

SPICED PUMPKIN PIE: To sugar mixture, stir in an additional ½ tsp. ground cinnamon and ½ tsp. ground nutmeg. With milk, stir in ½ tsp. vanilla and ½ tsp. maple flavoring.

PECAN PUMPKIN PIE: Pour filling into crust. Mix 2 lightly beaten large eggs, 1 cup chopped pecans, ½ cup sugar and ½ cup maple syrup; spoon over top.

1 PIECE: 369 cal., 13g fat (5g sat. fat), 81mg chol., 373mg sod., 60g carb. (39g sugars, 3g fiber), 6g pro.

"This pie is a breeze to make. My daughter Jessica says it's the best pumpkin pie she's ever eaten."
—JACKIE DEIBERT, KLINGERSTOWN, PA

PUMPKIN TORTE

This beautiful layered cake has a creamy pumpkin spice filling. It's quick and always turns out so well. The nuts and caramel topping add a nice finishing touch.

—TRIXIE FISHER, PIQUA, OH

PREP: 30 MIN. • **BAKE:** 25 MIN. + COOLING
MAKES: 12 SERVINGS

- 1 pkg. yellow cake mix (regular size)
- 1 can (15 oz.) solid-pack pumpkin, divided
- 4 large eggs
- ½ cup 2% milk
- ⅓ cup canola oil
- 1½ tsp. pumpkin pie spice, divided
- 1 pkg. (8 oz.) cream cheese, softened
- 1 cup confectioners' sugar
- 1 carton (16 oz.) frozen whipped topping, thawed
- ¼ cup caramel ice cream topping
  Pecan halves, toasted

1. Preheat oven to 350°. Line the bottoms of two greased 9-in. round baking pans with parchment paper; grease paper.

2. Combine cake mix, 1 cup pumpkin, eggs, milk, oil and 1 tsp. pie spice; beat on low speed 30 seconds. Beat on medium 2 minutes. Transfer to prepared pans.

3. Bake until a toothpick inserted in the center comes out clean, 25-30 minutes. Cool 10 minutes before removing from pans to wire racks; cool completely.

4. Beat cream cheese until light and fluffy. Beat in confectioners' sugar and the remaining pumpkin and pie spice until smooth. Fold in the whipped topping.

5. Using a long serrated knife, cut each cake horizontally in half. Place one cake layer on a serving plate; spread with a fourth of the filling. Repeat three times. Drizzle with caramel topping; sprinkle with pecans. Store in refrigerator.

1 SLICE: 476 cal., 24g fat (12g sat. fat), 82mg chol., 367mg sod., 58g carb. (41g sugars, 1g fiber), 6g pro.

HELPFUL HINT

When making the filling, be sure to fold in the whipped topping gently, just until it's blended. The filling will deflate if it's overhandled.

PUMPKIN CHOCOLATE CHIP CAKE

I have been baking this cake for friends and neighbors for years. Thanks to the totable pan, it's easy to make and take.

—KELLIE MOORE, FORT COLLINS, CO

PREP: 25 MIN. • **BAKE:** 20 MIN. + COOLING
MAKES: 15 SERVINGS

- 1¼ cups canned pumpkin
- 1 cup sugar
- ½ cup canola oil
- 2 large eggs
- 1 cup all-purpose flour
- 1 cup whole wheat flour
- 1½ tsp. baking powder
- ½ tsp. baking soda
- ½ tsp. salt
- 1¼ tsp. ground cinnamon
- ½ tsp. ground nutmeg
- ½ tsp. ground ginger
- ¼ tsp. ground cloves
- 1 cup semisweet chocolate chips

FROSTING

- 6 Tbsp. butter, softened
- 3 Tbsp. 2% milk
- 1½ tsp. vanilla extract
  Dash ground cloves, optional
- ⅓ cup baking cocoa
- 2½ to 3 cups confectioners' sugar
  Additional semisweet chocolate chips, optional

1. Preheat oven to 350°. Grease a 13x9-in. baking pan.

2. In a large bowl, beat pumpkin, sugar, oil and eggs until well blended. In another bowl, whisk flours, baking powder, baking soda, salt and spices; gradually beat into pumpkin mixture. Fold in chocolate chips.

3. Spread into the prepared baking pan. Bake 20-25 minutes or until a toothpick inserted in center comes out clean. Cool completely in pan on a wire rack.

4. Meanwhile, in a large bowl, beat butter until creamy. Beat in milk, vanilla and, if desired, cloves. Gradually beat in cocoa and enough of the confectioners' sugar to reach a spreading consistency. Spread over top of cake. If desired, sprinkle with additional chocolate chips.

1 PIECE: 374 cal., 17g fat (6g sat. fat), 37mg chol., 219mg sod., 56g carb. (40g sugars, 3g fiber), 4g pro.

CRANBERRY-PUMPKIN PRALINE PIE

Here's my spin on praline pie. It has a nice crunch from the pecans, brightness from orange zest, pop from the cranberries and richness from the cream cheese.

—BARB MILLER, OAKDALE, MN

PREP: 25 MIN. • **BAKE:** 50 MIN. + CHILLING
MAKES: 8 SERVINGS

- 12 oz. cream cheese, softened
- 1/3 cup sugar
- 1 large egg
- 1 1/2 tsp. grated orange zest
- Pastry for single-crust pie (9 in.)

PUMPKIN LAYER

- 1 can (15 oz.) solid-pack pumpkin
- 3/4 cup sugar
- 2 tsp. pumpkin pie spice
- 3 large eggs
- 3/4 cup half-and-half cream

CRANBERRY TOPPING

- 3/4 cup dried cranberries
- 3/4 cup chopped pecans
- 1/4 cup packed brown sugar
- 1 1/2 tsp. grated orange zest
- Whipped cream and ground nutmeg, optional

1. In small bowl, combine cream cheese and sugar; beat on medium speed until smooth. Beat in egg and orange zest. Refrigerate, covered, for 30 minutes.

2. Meanwhile, preheat oven to 375°. On a lightly floured surface, roll the dough to a 1/8-in.-thick circle; transfer to a 9-in. deep-dish pie plate. Trim pastry to 1/2 in. beyond rim of plate; flute edge. In a large bowl, combine pumpkin, sugar and pumpkin pie spice. Add eggs and cream; mix well.

3. Spread cream cheese mixture into pastry. Pour pumpkin mixture over cream cheese layer. Bake 25 minutes.

4. In a small bowl, combine the dried cranberries, pecans, brown sugar and orange zest. Sprinkle over pumpkin. Cover the edges with foil to prevent overbrowning. Bake 25-30 minutes longer or until a knife inserted in the center comes out clean. Cool on a wire rack.

5. Refrigerate for at least 2 hours. If desired, serve with whipped cream and nutmeg. Refrigerate leftovers.

1 PIECE: 596 cal., 35g fat (15g sat. fat), 169mg chol., 277mg sod., 64g carb. (45g sugars, 4g fiber), 10g pro.

PUMPKIN WALNUT CHEESECAKE

One of my friends gave me this recipe, and it has quickly become a family favorite. It's a perennial favorite at Thanksgiving. No one can eat just one slice!

—SUSAN GAROUTTE, GEORGETOWN, TX

PREP: 40 MIN.
BAKE: 1½ HOURS + CHILLING
MAKES: 12 SERVINGS

- 2 cups graham cracker crumbs
- ¼ cup sugar
- 6 Tbsp. butter, melted

FILLING

- 3 pkg. (8 oz. each) cream cheese, softened
- ¾ cup sugar
- ¾ cup packed dark brown sugar
- 1 can (15 oz.) solid-pack pumpkin
- ¼ cup heavy whipping cream
- 1 tsp. ground cinnamon
- 1 tsp. ground cloves
- 5 large eggs, lightly beaten

TOPPING

- 6 Tbsp. butter, softened
- 1 cup packed dark brown sugar
- 1 cup chopped walnuts

1. Place a greased 9-in. springform pan on a double thickness of heavy-duty foil (about 18 in. square). Wrap foil securely around pan. In a small bowl, combine cracker crumbs and sugar; stir in butter. Press onto the bottom and 1 in. up the sides of prepared pan.

2. In a large bowl, beat cream cheese and sugars until smooth. Beat in the pumpkin, cream, cinnamon and cloves until blended. Add eggs; beat on low speed just until combined. Pour over crust. Place springform pan in a large baking pan; add 1 in. of hot water to larger pan.

3. Bake at 325° for 1 hour. For topping, in a small bowl, combine butter and brown sugar. Stir in walnuts. Carefully sprinkle over hot cheesecake.

4. Bake 30 minutes longer or until center is just set. Remove springform pan from water bath. Cool on a wire rack for 10 minutes. Carefully run a knife around edge of pan to loosen; cool 1 hour longer. Refrigerate overnight. Remove sides of pan.

1 SLICE: 667 cal., 43g fat (22g sat. fat), 187mg chol., 379mg sod., 65g carb. (53g sugars, 3g fiber), 11g pro.

PUMPKIN MOUSSE PIE WITH GINGERSNAP CRUST

Gingersnaps and pumpkin taste so good together. This pie is a must-have dessert at our family get-togethers.
—**BERNICE JANOWSKI,**
STEVENS POINT, WI

PREP: 45 MIN. + CHILLING
MAKES: 8 SERVINGS

- 1½ **cups finely crushed gingersnap cookies (about 30 cookies)**
- 1 **cup finely chopped pecans, toasted**
- ⅓ **cup butter, melted**
- 1 **envelope unflavored gelatin**
- ¼ **cup cold water**
- ½ **cup packed brown sugar**
- ½ **cup half-and-half cream**
- 3 **large egg yolks**
- 1 **can (15 oz.) solid-pack pumpkin**
- 2 **tsp. pumpkin pie spice**
- 2 **cups whipped topping**
- ¼ **cup butterscotch-caramel ice cream topping**
- ½ **cup chopped pecans, toasted**

1. Preheat oven to 350°. In a small bowl, mix crushed cookies and chopped pecans; stir in butter. Press onto bottom and up sides of an ungreased 9-in. deep-dish pie plate. Bake 10-12 minutes or until lightly browned. Cool on a wire rack.

2. In a microwave-safe bowl, sprinkle gelatin over cold water; let stand for 1 minute. Microwave this mixture on high for 30-40 seconds. Stir. Let stand for 1 minute or until the gelatin is completely dissolved.

3. In a large saucepan, whisk brown sugar, cream and egg yolks until blended. Cook over low heat until a thermometer reads at least 160°, stirring constantly. (Do not allow to boil.) Remove from heat; stir in pumpkin, pie spice and gelatin mixture. Cool completely.

4. Fold in the whipped topping. Pour into crust; refrigerate until set. Drizzle with ice cream topping and sprinkle with pecans.

NOTE To toast pecans, bake in a shallow pan in a 350° oven for 5-10 minutes or cook in a skillet over low heat until lightly browned, stirring occasionally.

1 PIECE: 516 cal., 32g fat (12g sat. fat), 98mg chol., 227mg sod., 53g carb. (28g sugars, 4g fiber), 7g pro.

HELPFUL HINT

To crush and measure cookies without making a mess, place them in a resealable plastic bag and crush with a rolling pin or can. Then smoosh the bag of crumbs into a liquid measuring cup to see how much you have.

GIANT CUPCAKE PUMPKIN

Make a smiley statement by decorating a whole tray of chocolate spice cupcakes. Once everyone's seen the big picture, they can each take a treat.

—GENA LOTT, OGDEN, UT

PREP: 35 MIN. • **BAKE:** 20 MIN. + COOLING
MAKES: 26 CUPCAKES

- 1 pkg. spice cake mix (regular size)
- 1 cup solid-pack pumpkin
- 1 cup water
- 2 large eggs
- 1 cup miniature semisweet chocolate chips
- 2 cans (16 oz. each) vanilla frosting
- 1 tsp. maple flavoring
  Orange food coloring
  Reese's Pieces

1. Preheat oven to 350°. Line 26 muffin cups with paper liners.

2. In a large bowl, combine cake mix, pumpkin, water and eggs; beat on low speed 30 seconds. Beat on medium for 2 minutes. Stir in chocolate chips. Fill prepared cups two-thirds full.

3. Bake for 16-20 minutes or until a toothpick inserted in the center comes out clean. Cool in pans 10 minutes before removing to wire racks to cool completely.

4. In a large bowl, beat frosting and flavoring; tint frosting orange. Arrange cupcakes on a large platter, forming a pumpkin. Spread frosting over cupcakes. Decorate with Reese's Pieces as desired.

1 CUPCAKE: 256 cal., 8g fat (4g sat. fat), 14mg chol., 215mg sod., 44g carb. (32g sugars, 1g fiber), 2g pro.

NOTES

PRALINE PUMPKIN TORTE

Perfect for an autumn day, this torte is decadent to the last bite.

—**ESTHER SINN, PRINCETON, IL**

PREP: 25 MIN. • **BAKE:** 30 MIN. + COOLING
MAKES: 14 SERVINGS

- ¾ cup packed brown sugar
- ⅓ cup butter
- 3 Tbsp. heavy whipping cream
- ¾ cup chopped pecans

CAKE

- 4 large eggs
- 1⅔ cups sugar
- 1 cup canola oil
- 2 cups canned pumpkin
- ¼ tsp. vanilla extract
- 2 cups all-purpose flour
- 2 tsp. baking powder
- 2 tsp. pumpkin pie spice
- 1 tsp. baking soda
- 1 tsp. salt

TOPPING

- 1¾ cups heavy whipping cream
- ¼ cup confectioners' sugar
- ¼ tsp. vanilla extract
  Additional chopped pecans, optional

1. In a heavy saucepan, combine the brown sugar, butter and cream. Cook and stir over low heat until sugar is dissolved. Pour into two well-greased 9-in. round baking pans. Sprinkle with pecans; cool.

2. For cake, in a large bowl, beat the eggs, sugar and oil. Add pumpkin and vanilla. Combine the flour, baking powder, pie spice, baking soda and salt; gradually add to pumpkin mixture just until blended.

3. Carefully spoon batter over the brown sugar mixture. Bake at 350° for 30-35 minutes or until a toothpick inserted in the center comes out clean. Cool 5 minutes; remove from pans to wire racks to cool completely.

4. For topping, in a small bowl, beat cream until it begins to thicken. Add confectioners' sugar and vanilla; beat until stiff peaks form.

5. Place one cake layer, praline side up, on a serving plate. Spread two-thirds of the whipped cream mixture over cake. Top with second cake layer and remaining whipped cream. Sprinkle with additional pecans if desired. Store torte in the refrigerator.

1 PIECE: 577 cal., 38g fat (13g sat. fat), 118mg chol., 397mg sod., 56g carb. (39g sugars, 3g fiber), 6g pro.

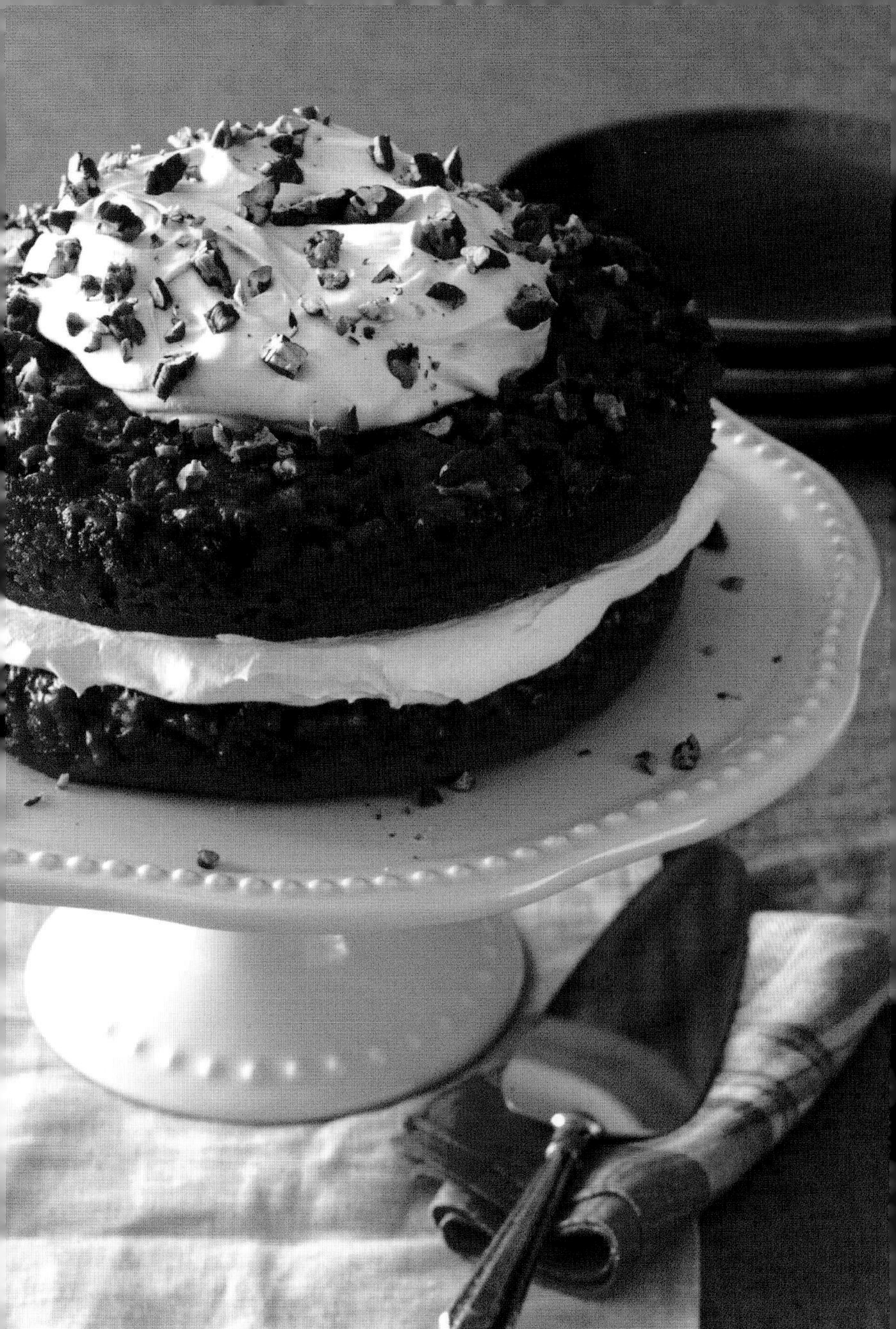

MOM'S BEST PUMPKIN CHEESECAKE

Pumpkin swirls not only turn this fall cheesecake into a show-stopper, they also make it more delicious!

—JAMI GEITTMANN, GREENDALE, WI

PREP: 35 MIN. • BAKE: 55 MIN. + CHILLING
MAKES: 12 SERVINGS

- 1½ cups graham cracker crumbs
- ¼ cup sugar
- ⅓ cup butter, melted

FILLING
- 4 pkg. (8 oz. each) cream cheese, softened
- 1½ cups sugar
- 2 Tbsp. cornstarch
- 2 tsp. vanilla extract
- 4 large eggs
- 1 cup canned pumpkin
- 2 tsp. ground cinnamon
- 1½ tsp. ground nutmeg

TOPPINGS
- Whipped cream, additional ground cinnamon and caramel syrup, optional

1. Preheat oven to 325°. Place a greased 9-in. springform pan on a double thickness of heavy-duty foil (about 18 in. square). Securely wrap foil around pan.

2. Combine crumbs and ¼ cup of sugar; stir in butter. Press onto bottom and 1½ in. up the sides of prepared pan. Place on a baking sheet. Bake until set, 10-15 minutes. Cool on a wire rack.

3. For the filling, beat 1 package of cream cheese, ½ cup sugar and the cornstarch until smooth, about 2 minutes. Beat in remaining cream cheese, one package at a time, until smooth. Beat in remaining sugar and vanilla. Add eggs; beat on low speed just until combined. Place 2 cups filling in a small bowl; stir in pumpkin, cinnamon and nutmeg.

4. Pour half of plain filling over crust; dollop with half of pumpkin filling. Cut through with a knife to swirl. Repeat layers and swirling.

5. Place springform pan in a large baking pan; add 1 in. of hot water to larger pan. Bake 55-65 minutes or until center is just set and top appears dull. Remove springform pan from water bath. Cool on a wire rack for 10 minutes. Carefully run a knife around edge of pan to loosen; cool 1 hour longer. Refrigerate overnight, covering when completely cooled. Remove rim from pan. If desired, top with whipped cream and cinnamon or caramel sauce.

1 SLICE: 518 cal., 34g fat (19g sat. fat), 152mg chol., 361mg sod., 47g carb. (36g sugars, 1g fiber), 8g pro.

GINGER-STREUSEL PUMPKIN PIE

I love to bake and have spent a lot of time making goodies for my family and friends. The streusel topping gives this pie a special touch your family will love.

—SONIA PARVU, SHERRILL, NY

PREP: 25 MIN. • **BAKE:** 55 MIN. + COOLING • **MAKES:** 8 SERVINGS

- 1 sheet refrigerated pie crust
- 3 large eggs
- 1 can (15 oz.) solid-pack pumpkin
- 1½ cups heavy whipping cream
- ½ cup sugar
- ¼ cup packed brown sugar
- 1½ tsp. ground cinnamon
- ½ tsp. salt
- ¼ tsp. ground allspice
- ¼ tsp. ground nutmeg
- ¼ tsp. ground cloves

STREUSEL

- 1 cup all-purpose flour
- ½ cup packed brown sugar
- ½ cup cold butter, cubed
- ½ cup chopped walnuts
- ⅓ cup finely chopped crystallized ginger

1. Preheat oven to 350°. On a lightly floured surface, unroll crust. Transfer to a 9-in. pie plate and trim to ½ in. beyond edge of plate; flute edges.

2. In a large bowl, whisk eggs, pumpkin, cream, sugars, cinnamon, salt, allspice, nutmeg and cloves. Pour into crust. Bake 40 minutes.

3. In a small bowl, combine flour and brown sugar; cut in butter until crumbly. Stir in walnuts and ginger. Gently sprinkle over filling.

4. Bake 15-25 minutes longer or until a knife inserted in the center of the pie comes out clean. Cool on a wire rack. Refrigerate the leftovers.

1 PIECE: 684 cal., 42g fat (21g sat. fat), 176mg chol., 388mg sod., 73g carb. (39g sugars, 3g fiber), 9g pro.

CONTEST-WINNING PUMPKIN CHEESECAKE DESSERT

With its gingersnap crust and maple syrup drizzle, this rich and creamy spiced pumpkin dessert never fails to get rave reviews. It cuts nicely, too.

—CATHY HALL, LYNDHURST, VA

PREP: 25 MIN. • **BAKE:** 40 MIN. + CHILLING • **MAKES:** 24 SERVINGS

- 1½ cups crushed gingersnaps (about 30 cookies)
- ¼ cup butter, melted
- 5 pkg. (8 oz. each) cream cheese, softened
- 1 cup sugar
- 1 can (15 oz.) solid-pack pumpkin
- 1 tsp. ground cinnamon
- 1 tsp. vanilla extract
- 5 large eggs, lightly beaten
  Ground nutmeg
  Maple syrup
  Sweetened whipped cream, optional

1. In a small bowl, combine gingersnap crumbs and melted butter. Press onto bottom of a greased 13x9-in. baking dish; set aside.

2. In a large bowl, beat cream cheese and sugar until smooth. Beat in the pumpkin, cinnamon and vanilla. Add eggs; beat on low speed just until combined. Pour over crust; sprinkle with nutmeg.

3. Bake at 350° for 40-45 minutes or until center is almost set. Cool on a wire rack for 10 minutes. Carefully run a knife around edge of baking dish to loosen; cool 1 hour longer. Refrigerate overnight.

4. Cut into squares; serve with maple syrup and, if desired, sweetened whipped cream. Refrigerate leftovers.

1 PIECE: 143 cal., 7g fat (4g sat. fat), 60mg chol., 122mg sod., 17g carb. (12g sugars, 1g fiber), 3g pro.

EGGNOG PUMPKIN PIE

This family favorite is a combination of our favorite holiday flavors. With its flaky crust, creamy filling and crunchy topping, it's the perfect finale to a special meal.

**—LYN DILWORTH,
RANCHO CORDOVA, CA**

PREP: 40 MIN. + CHILLING
BAKE: 50 MIN. + COOLING
MAKES: 8 SERVINGS

1¼ cups all-purpose flour
¼ tsp. salt
3 Tbsp. shortening, cubed
3 Tbsp. cold butter, cubed
3 to 4 Tbsp. cold water

FILLING

2 large eggs
1 can (15 oz.) solid-pack pumpkin
1 cup eggnog
½ cup sugar
1 tsp. ground cinnamon
½ tsp. salt
½ tsp. ground ginger
½ tsp. ground nutmeg
¼ tsp. ground cloves

TOPPING

½ cup packed brown sugar
2 Tbsp. butter, softened
½ cup chopped pecans

1. In a food processor, combine flour and salt; cover and pulse to blend. Add shortening and butter; cover and pulse until mixture resembles coarse crumbs. While processing, gradually add water until dough forms a ball. Wrap dough in plastic. Refrigerate for 1-1½ hours or until easy to handle.

2. Roll out pastry to fit a 9-in. pie plate. Transfer to pie plate and trim to ½ in. beyond edge of plate; flute the edges.

3. In a large bowl, whisk the eggs, pumpkin, eggnog, sugar, cinnamon, salt, ginger, nutmeg and cloves until blended. Pour into crust.

4. In a small bowl, beat the brown sugar and butter until crumbly, about 2 minutes. Stir in the pecans; sprinkle mixture over filling.

5. Bake at 350° for 50-60 minutes or until a knife inserted in the center comes out clean. Cool on a wire rack. Refrigerate leftovers.

NOTE This recipe was tested with commercially prepared eggnog.

1 PIECE: 408 cal., 21g fat (8g sat. fat), 90mg chol., 315mg sod., 51g carb. (31g sugars, 4g fiber), 6g pro.

MINI PUMPKIN PRALINE POUND CAKES

My family's favorite holiday dessert is a real southern treat. A warm praline sauce and sprinkling of pecans make each small pound cake even more decadent.

—DIANE HILL ROARK, BENTON, AR

PREP: 20 MIN. • **BAKE:** 20 MIN + COOLING
MAKES: 6 LOAVES (3 SLICES EACH)

2½ cups all-purpose flour
1 tsp. salt
1 tsp. baking soda
1 tsp. ground cinnamon
1 tsp. ground nutmeg
½ tsp. ground cloves
¼ tsp. ground ginger
2 cups canned pumpkin
4 large eggs
2 cups sugar
½ cup canola oil
½ cup butter, melted

PRALINE SAUCE
1 cup packed brown sugar
¼ cup butter
¼ cup heavy whipping cream
1 cup chopped pecans

1. In a large bowl, combine the first seven ingredients. In another bowl, beat the pumpkin, eggs, sugar, oil and butter until well blended. Gradually stir into dry ingredients just until blended.

2. Transfer to six greased and floured 5¾x3x2-in. loaf pans. Bake at 350° for 20-25 minutes or until a toothpick inserted in the center comes out clean. Cool for 10 minutes before removing from pans to wire racks to cool completely.

3. For sauce, in a small saucepan, combine the brown sugar, butter and cream. Cook and stir over medium heat until sugar is dissolved. Pour over cakes; top with pecans.

1 SLICE: 399 cal., 21g fat (7g sat. fat), 65mg chol., 284mg sod., 51g carb. (36g sugars, 2g fiber), 4g pro.

PUMPKIN CUPCAKES WITH SPICED FROSTING

My aunt makes the most delicious pumpkin pies for Thanksgiving, but my kids prefer cupcakes for dessert, so I created these for the youngsters at our holiday table.
—AIMEE SHUGARMAN, LIBERTY TOWNSHIP, OH

PREP: 15 MIN. • **BAKE:** 25 MIN. + COOLING • **MAKES:** 1 DOZEN

- 1 cup canned pumpkin
- 2 large eggs
- ½ cup sugar
- ½ cup packed brown sugar
- ¼ cup unsweetened applesauce
- ¼ cup canola oil
- 1 cup all-purpose flour
- 1 tsp. baking powder
- ½ tsp. baking soda
- ¼ tsp. salt
- 1½ tsp. ground cinnamon
- 1½ tsp. pumpkin pie spice

FROSTING

- 1 can (16 oz.) vanilla frosting
- 1 cup whipped topping
- 1 tsp. ground cinnamon
  Candy corn

1. Preheat oven to 350°. Line 12 muffin cups with paper or foil liners. Beat first six ingredients until well blended. In another bowl, whisk flour, baking powder, baking soda, salt and spices; gradually beat into pumpkin mixture.

2. Fill prepared cups two-thirds full. Bake until a toothpick inserted in the center comes out clean, 25-30 minutes. Cool cupcakes in pans 10 minutes before removing to wire racks to cool completely.

3. Mix frosting, whipped topping and cinnamon. Pipe or spoon onto cupcakes; top with candy corn. Refrigerate the leftovers.

1 CUPCAKE: 359 cal., 12g fat (5g sat. fat), 31mg chol., 238mg sod., 59g carb. (45g sugars, 1g fiber), 2g pro.

MAPLE-KISSED PUMPKIN PIE

We make our own maple syrup, and that's what gives this pie its special taste. Go ahead and bake this to go with your Thanksgiving meal.

—MARTHA BOUDAH, ESSEX CENTER, VT

PREP: 10 MIN. + CHILLING
BAKE: 1 HOUR + COOLING
MAKES: 8 SERVINGS

- 1 can (15 oz.) solid-pack pumpkin
- 2 Tbsp. all-purpose flour
- ½ tsp. ground cinnamon
- ½ tsp. ground nutmeg
- ½ tsp. ground ginger
- 1 Tbsp. butter, softened
- 1 cup sugar
- 1 cup whole milk
- 2 Tbsp. maple syrup
- 2 large eggs
- 1 unbaked pie shell (9 in.)
  Whipped cream, optional

In a bowl, combine first 10 ingredients. Pour into the pie shell. Bake at 425° for 15 minutes. Reduce heat to 350° and continue baking for about 45 minutes or until a knife inserted in center comes out clean. Cool to room temperature, then refrigerate. Garnish with whipped cream if desired.

1 PIECE: 308 cal., 11g fat (5g sat. fat), 66mg chol., 148mg sod., 49g carb. (32g sugars, 3g fiber), 5g pro.

PUMPKIN CAKE WITH CARAMEL SAUCE

If a recipe has pumpkin in it, it's likely I'll enjoy it! This one resulted when I added a favorite key ingredient to an old spice-cake recipe that I had. Everyone who's tried it has enjoyed it.

—ROBERTA PECK, FORT HILL, PA

PREP: 20 MIN. • **BAKE:** 40 MIN. + COOLING
MAKES: 16 SERVINGS

- 2 cups all-purpose flour
- 2 cups sugar
- 2 tsp. ground cinnamon
- 1 tsp. baking soda
- 1 tsp. ground nutmeg
- ½ tsp. salt
- 4 large eggs
- 1 can (15 oz.) solid-pack pumpkin
- 1 cup canola oil

CARAMEL SAUCE

- 1½ cups packed brown sugar
- 3 Tbsp. all-purpose flour
  Dash salt
- 1¼ cups water
- 2 Tbsp. butter
- ½ tsp. vanilla extract

1. In a large bowl, combine flour, sugar, cinnamon, baking soda, nutmeg and salt. In another bowl, beat the eggs, pumpkin and oil until smooth; add to the dry ingredients. Mix until well blended, about 1 minute.

2. Pour the batter into a greased 13x9-in. baking pan. Bake at 350° for 40-45 minutes or until a toothpick inserted in center comes out clean. Cool on a wire rack.

3. For sauce, combine the brown sugar, flour and salt in a small saucepan. Stir in water and butter; bring to a boil over medium heat. Boil for 3 minutes, stirring constantly. Remove from the heat; stir in vanilla. Cut cake into squares and serve with warm sauce.

1 SERVING: 425 cal., 18g fat (3g sat. fat), 61mg chol., 215mg sod., 65g carb. (49g sugars, 2g fiber), 4g pro.

HELPFUL HINT

Dark brown sugar contains more molasses than light or golden brown sugar. These types are generally interchangeable in recipes. If you prefer a bolder flavor, choose dark brown.

MOIST PUMPKIN BUNDT CAKE

This cake is perfect for fall. As it bakes, the aroma fills the house with a spicy scent.
—VIRGINIA LOEW, LEESBURG, FL

PREP: 10 MIN. • **BAKE:** 1 HOUR + COOLING
MAKES: 16 SERVINGS

- 2½ cups sugar
- 1 cup canola oil
- 3 large eggs
- 3 cups all-purpose flour
- 2 tsp. baking soda
- 1 tsp. ground cinnamon
- 1 tsp. ground nutmeg
- ½ tsp. salt
- ¼ tsp. ground cloves
- 1 can (15 oz.) solid-pack pumpkin
  Confectioners' sugar

1. Preheat oven to 350°. In a large bowl, combine the sugar and oil until blended. Add eggs, one at a time, beating well after each addition. Combine flour, baking soda, cinnamon, nutmeg, salt and cloves; add to egg mixture alternately with pumpkin, beating well after each addition.

2. Transfer to a greased 10-in. fluted tube pan. Bake 60-65 minutes or until toothpick inserted in the center comes out clean. Cool for 10 minutes before inverting onto a wire rack. Remove cake from pan and cool completely. Dust with confectioners' sugar.

1 SLICE: 351 cal., 15g fat (2g sat. fat), 40mg chol., 245mg sod., 51g carb. (32g sugars, 2g fiber), 4g pro.

PUMPKIN GINGERSNAP ICE CREAM PIE

My family and I always try new desserts during the holidays. This one was a clear winner at our Christmas party, so now we make it for all of our special occasions!

—PATRICIA NESS, LA MESA, CA

PREP: 25 MIN. + FREEZING • **MAKES:** 8 SERVINGS

1½ cups crushed gingersnaps (about 30 cookies)
2 Tbsp. ground walnuts
1 Tbsp. canola oil

FILLING

4 cups reduced-fat vanilla ice cream, softened if necessary
1 cup canned pumpkin pie filling
Pumpkin pie spice

1. Preheat oven to 350°. In a small bowl, mix crushed cookies and walnuts; stir in oil. Press onto bottom and up the sides of an ungreased 9-in. pie plate. Bake for 8-10 minutes or until set. Cool completely on a wire rack.

2. In a large bowl, mix ice cream and pie filling until blended. Spread into prepared crust; sprinkle with pumpkin pie spice. Freeze, covered, 8 hours or overnight.

1 PIECE: 304 cal., 9g fat (3g sat. fat), 21mg chol., 233mg sod., 50g carb. (29g sugars, 2g fiber), 6g pro.

MARSHMALLOW PUMPKIN PIE

PREP: 20 MIN. + CHILLING • **MAKES:** 8 SERVINGS

- **1 pkg. (10 oz.) large marshmallows**
- **1 cup canned pumpkin**
- **1 tsp. ground cinnamon**
- **½ tsp. salt**
- **½ tsp. ground ginger**
- **½ tsp. ground nutmeg**
- **2 cups whipped topping**
- **1 graham cracker crust (9 in.)**
- **Additional whipped topping, optional**

1. In a large saucepan, combine the first six ingredients; cook and stir over medium heat 8-10 minutes or until marshmallows are melted. Remove from heat; cool to room temperature.

2. Fold in whipped topping. Spoon into crust. Refrigerate 3 hours or until set. If desired, serve pie with additional whipped topping.

1 PIECE: 280 cal., 9g fat (4g sat. fat), 0 chol., 287mg sod., 49g carb. (33g sugars, 2g fiber), 2g pro.

"This was one of my mother's favorite pies. She was a great cook and was always generous with her recipes. The filling also tastes great in baked pastry crust or gingersnap crust."

—RUTH FERRIS, BILLINGS, MT

CHOCOLATE CHIP PUMPKIN CAKE

It's surprising how perfectly chocolate and pumpkin combine in this pretty, two-toned cake. The flavorful blend really does take the cake!

—LAURENE HUNSICKER, CANTON, PA

PREP: 30 MIN. • **BAKE:** 65 MIN. + COOLING
MAKES: 12 SERVINGS

- ¾ **cup butter, softened**
- 1½ **cups sugar**
- ½ **cup packed brown sugar**
- 2 **large eggs**
- 1 **tsp. vanilla extract**
- 2½ **cups all-purpose flour**
- 1 **tsp. baking powder**
- 1 **tsp. baking soda**
- 1 **tsp. ground cinnamon**
- 1 **can (15 oz.) solid-pack pumpkin**
- 1 **cup semisweet chocolate chips**
- 2 **oz. unsweetened chocolate, melted and cooled**
- ¾ **cup finely chopped pecans, divided**

1. In a large bowl, cream butter and sugars until light and fluffy. Add the eggs, one at a time, beating well after each addition. Beat in vanilla. Combine the flour, baking powder, baking soda and cinnamon; add to the creamed mixture alternately with pumpkin, beating well after each addition. Fold in chocolate chips.

2. Divide batter in half. Stir melted chocolate into one portion. In a well-greased 10-in. fluted tube pan, sprinkle ½ cup pecans. Spoon chocolate batter over pecans; top with pumpkin batter. Sprinkle with remaining pecans.

3. Bake at 325° for 65-70 minutes or until a toothpick inserted in the center comes out clean. Cool for 15 minutes before removing from pan to a wire rack.

1 SLICE: 494 cal., 25g fat (12g sat. fat), 65mg chol., 239mg sod., 68g carb. (44g sugars, 5g fiber), 6g pro.

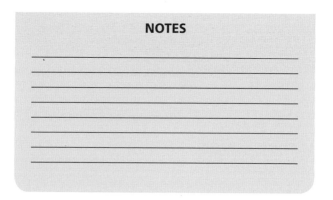

NOTES

SURPRISE PUMPKIN CUPCAKES

Cupcakes are the perfect workplace treat because they're already wrapped up and so easy to eat.

—KATHLEEN DIMMICH, EASTON, PA

PREP: 25 MIN. • **BAKE:** 20 MIN. + COOLING • **MAKES:** 2 DOZEN

- 1 can (15 oz.) solid-pack pumpkin
- 2 cups sugar
- 1 cup canola oil
- 4 large eggs
- 2 cups all-purpose flour
- 2 tsp. baking powder
- 2 tsp. ground cinnamon
- 1 tsp. baking soda
- ½ tsp. salt

FILLING

- 1 pkg. (8 oz.) cream cheese, softened
- ⅓ cup sugar
- 1 large egg
  Confectioners' sugar, optional

1. In a large bowl, beat the pumpkin, sugar, oil and eggs until well blended. In small bowl, combine the flour, baking powder, cinnamon, baking soda and salt; gradually beat into pumpkin mixture until blended.

2. For the filling, in another small bowl, beat cream cheese and sugar until smooth. Add egg; beat together on low just until combined.

3. Fill 24 paper-lined muffin cups one-third full. Drop filling by tablespoonfuls into center of each cupcake. Cover with remaining batter.

4. Bake at 350° for 20-25 minutes or until a toothpick inserted in the pumpkin portion comes out clean. Cool for 10 minutes before removing from pans to wire racks to cool completely. Dust with confectioners' sugar if desired. Refrigerate leftovers.

1 CUPCAKE: 250 cal., 14g fat (3g sat. fat), 54mg chol., 179mg sod., 29g carb. (20g sugars, 1g fiber), 3g pro.

CHOCOLATE PUMPKIN SPIDERWEB TART

Guests are sure to get caught up in this creamy pumpkin and chocolate swirled tart. The fancy web pattern is easy to create and so impressive.

—*TASTE OF HOME* TEST KITCHEN

PREP: 30 MIN. • **BAKE:** 30 MIN. + CHILLING
MAKES: 14 SERVINGS

- **2 cups chocolate graham cracker crumbs (about 14 whole crackers)**
- **½ cup sugar**
- **½ cup butter, melted**

FILLING

- **1½ cups canned pumpkin**
- **¾ cup sugar**
- **4 oz. cream cheese, softened**
- **1¼ cups heavy whipping cream**
- **1 tsp. grated orange zest**
- **½ tsp. ground ginger**
- **½ tsp. ground cinnamon**
- **¼ tsp. salt**
- **¼ tsp. ground nutmeg**
- **3 large eggs, lightly beaten**
- **4½ tsp. baking cocoa**
   Chopped glazed walnuts, optional

1. Preheat oven to 350°. Combine cracker crumbs, sugar and butter. Press onto the bottom and up the sides of an ungreased 11-in. fluted tart pan with removable bottom. Place pan on a baking sheet; bake 8 minutes. Cool on a wire rack. Increase oven setting to 375°.

2. Meanwhile, beat pumpkin, sugar and cream cheese until blended. Beat in the next six ingredients. Add the eggs; beat on low speed just until combined. Transfer ¾ cup filling to a small bowl; whisk in cocoa.

3. Pour pumpkin filling into crust. Transfer the chocolate mixture to a heavy-duty resealable plastic bag; cut a small hole in a corner of bag. Pipe 4 concentric circles 1 in. apart over filling. Beginning with center circle, gently pull a knife through all four circles toward outer edge. Wipe the knife clean. Repeat to complete the spiderweb pattern.

4. Bake until set, 28-33 minutes. Cool for 1 hour; refrigerate overnight. If desired, serve with glazed walnuts.

1 SLICE: 321 cal., 20g fat (11g sat. fat), 90mg chol., 237mg sod., 34g carb. (24g sugars, 1g fiber), 4g pro.

PUMPKIN-PECAN SPICE CAKE

I'm a wife and a mother of eight children. I like baking more than cooking, so I enjoy dressing up cake mix with nuts, canned pumpkin and a homemade cream cheese frosting to create this fabulous dessert.

—JOYCE PLATFOOT, WAPAKONETA, OH

PREP: 25 MIN. • **BAKE:** 30 MIN. + COOLING
MAKES: 20 SERVINGS

- 2 cups crushed vanilla wafers (about 60 wafers)
- 1 cup chopped pecans
- ¾ cup butter, softened

CAKE

- 1 pkg. spice cake mix (regular size)
- 1 can (15 oz.) solid-pack pumpkin
- 4 large eggs
- ½ cup butter, softened

FILLING

- 6 oz. cream cheese, softened
- 1⅓ cups butter, softened
- 6 cups confectioners' sugar
- 4 tsp. vanilla extract

TOPPING

- ½ cup caramel ice cream topping
  Pecan halves

1. In a large bowl, combine wafers, pecans and butter until crumbly. Press into three greased and floured 9-in. round baking pans.
2. For cake, in another large bowl, beat the cake mix, pumpkin, eggs and butter; beat on low speed for 30 seconds. Beat on high speed for 2 minutes. Spread over the crust in each pan.
3. Bake at 350° for 30 minutes or until a toothpick inserted in center comes out clean. Cool in pans for 10 minutes before removing to wire racks to cool completely.
4. For filling, in a small bowl, beat cream cheese and butter until fluffy. Add confectioners' sugar and vanilla; beat until smooth.
5. Spread filling between the layers (crumb side down) and on the sides and top of cake. Spread caramel topping over top, allowing some to drip down the sides. Garnish with pecan halves. Store in refrigerator.

1 PIECE: 614 cal., 36g fat (18g sat. fat), 111mg chol., 471mg sod., 72g carb. (56g sugars, 2g fiber), 4g pro.

PUMPKIN
SWEETS

PUMPKIN BARS

PREP: 20 MIN. • **BAKE:** 25 MIN. + COOLING • **MAKES:** 2 DOZEN

- 4 large eggs
- 1⅔ cups sugar
- 1 cup canola oil
- 1 can (15 oz.) solid-pack pumpkin
- 2 cups all-purpose flour
- 2 tsp. ground cinnamon
- 2 tsp. baking powder
- 1 tsp. baking soda
- 1 tsp. salt

ICING
- 6 oz. cream cheese, softened
- 2 cups confectioners' sugar
- ¼ cup butter, softened
- 1 tsp. vanilla extract
- 1 to 2 Tbsp. whole milk

1. In a bowl, beat the eggs, sugar, oil and pumpkin until well blended. Combine the flour, cinnamon, baking powder, baking soda and salt; gradually add to pumpkin mixture and mix well. Pour into an ungreased 15x10x1-in. baking pan. Bake at 350° for 25-30 minutes or until set. Cool completely.

2. For icing, beat the cream cheese, confectioners' sugar, butter and vanilla in a small bowl. Add enough milk to achieve spreading consistency. Spread over bars. Store in the refrigerator.

1 BAR: 260 cal., 13g fat (3g sat. fat), 45mg chol., 226mg sod., 34g carb. (24g sugars, 1g fiber), 3g pro.

"What could be a more appropriate fall treat than a big pan of pumpkin-flavored bars? Actually, my family loves these any time of year. "

—BRENDA KELLER, ANDALUSIA, AL

PUMPKIN SPICE CUTOUTS

Through all the years I've been baking, I've never come across a pumpkin cookie recipe that you can actually cut out with cookie cutters. (Most I've found are drop cookies.) Each bite tastes just like pumpkin pie—delicious!

—MARION KEARLEY, LADNER, BC

PREP: 20 MIN. + CHILLING
BAKE: 10 MIN./BATCH + COOLING
MAKES: 3 DOZEN

- ½ cup shortening
- ¾ cup granulated sugar
- ½ cup canned pumpkin pie mix
- ¼ cup molasses
- 3 cups all-purpose flour
- 1 tsp. baking soda
- 1 tsp. ground ginger
- 1 tsp. ground cinnamon
- ½ tsp. baking powder
- ½ tsp. salt

ICING
- 4 cups confectioners' sugar
- ⅓ cup butter, softened
- 3 to 4 Tbsp. 2% milk
  Food coloring, optional

1. Cream shortening and sugar until light and fluffy. Beat in pumpkin pie mix and molasses. In another bowl, whisk next six ingredients; gradually beat into creamed mixture. Divide dough in half. Shape each into a disk; wrap in plastic. Refrigerate several hours, until firm enough to roll.

2. Preheat oven to 375°. On a lightly floured surface, roll each portion of dough to ¼-in. thickness. Cut with floured 2½-in. pumpkin-shaped cookie cutters. Place 2 in. apart on greased baking sheets. Bake until edges are firm, 8-10 minutes. Remove cookies from pans to wire racks to cool completely.

3. For icing, beat confectioners' sugar, butter and enough milk to reach spreading consistency. If desired, tint with food coloring. Decorate cookies as desired.

1 COOKIE: 156 cal., 5g fat (2g sat. fat), 5mg chol., 94mg sod., 28g carb. (20g sugars, 0 fiber), 1g pro.

PUMPKIN-CREAM CHEESE ICE CREAM

Everyone loves a pumpkin-flavored cheesecake, but we decided to make a cool ice cream version. We're quite pleased with the result.
—*TASTE OF HOME* TEST KITCHEN

PREP: 30 MIN. + FREEZING • **MAKES:** ABOUT 1 QT.

- 2 cups heavy whipping cream
- 1 pkg. (8 oz.) cream cheese, cubed
- ¾ cup packed brown sugar
- 5 large egg yolks
- 1 tsp. salt
- 1 tsp. ground cinnamon
- ½ tsp. ground ginger
- ½ tsp. ground nutmeg
- 1 cup canned pumpkin
- 1 tsp. vanilla extract

1. In a large heavy saucepan, heat 1½ cups cream, cream cheese and ½ cup brown sugar until bubbles form around sides of pan. Meanwhile, in a small bowl, whisk the egg yolks, salt, spices and the remaining cream and brown sugar. Whisk a small amount of hot mixture into the eggs. Return all to the pan, whisking constantly.

2. Cook and stir over low heat until mixture is thickened and coats the back of a spoon. Quickly strain through a fine-mesh sieve into a bowl; place in ice water and stir for 2 minutes. Whisk in pumpkin and vanilla. Continue to whisk until completely cooled.

3. Fill cylinder of ice cream freezer two-thirds full; freeze according to the manufacturer's directions. When ice cream is frozen, transfer to a freezer container; freeze for 2-4 hours before serving.

½ **CUP:** 430 cal., 34g fat (21g sat. fat), 212mg chol., 413mg sod., 27g carb. (24g sugars, 1g fiber), 6g pro.

GINGERBREAD & PUMPKIN CREAM TRIFLE

We wait for these flavors all year long. Stack the layers in a big trifle bowl, or make minis for everybody at the table.

—AMY GEISER, FAIRLAWN, OH

PREP: 45 MIN. + CHILLING • **MAKES:** 10 SERVINGS

- 1 pkg. (14½ oz.) gingerbread cake/cookie mix
- 1 pkg. (3 oz.) cook-and-serve vanilla pudding mix
- ¼ cup packed brown sugar
- 1⅔ cups canned pumpkin pie mix
- 1 carton (8 oz.) frozen whipped topping, thawed
  Optional toppings: caramel topping, toasted pecans and gingersnap cookies

1. Prepare and bake gingerbread cake according to the package directions. Cool completely on a wire rack.

2. Meanwhile, prepare pudding mix according to package directions; stir in brown sugar and pie mix. Transfer to a bowl; refrigerate, covered, for 30 minutes.

3. Cut or break gingerbread into ¾-in. pieces. In ten 12-oz. glasses or a 3-qt. trifle bowl, layer half of each of the following: cake, pumpkin mixture and whipped topping. Repeat layers. Refrigerate, covered, 4 hours or overnight. Top as desired.

1 SERVING: 372 cal., 11g fat (6g sat. fat), 23mg chol., 414mg sod., 61g carb. (44g sugars, 2g fiber), 5g pro.

PUMPKIN CRANBERRY BREAD PUDDING

Savor your favorite fall flavors with this scrumptious bread pudding, served warm with a sweet vanilla sauce. Yum!

—JUDITH BUCCIARELLI, NEWBURGH, NY

PREP: 15 MIN. • **COOK:** 3 HOURS
MAKES: 8 SERVINGS (1⅓ CUPS SAUCE)

- 8 slices cinnamon bread, cut into 1-in. cubes
- 4 large eggs, beaten
- 2 cups 2% milk
- 1 cup canned pumpkin
- ¼ cup packed brown sugar
- ¼ cup butter, melted
- 1 tsp. vanilla extract
- ½ tsp. ground cinnamon
- ¼ tsp. ground nutmeg
- ½ cup dried cranberries

SAUCE
- 1 cup granulated sugar
- ⅔ cup water
- 1 cup heavy whipping cream
- 2 tsp. vanilla extract
  Vanilla ice cream, optional

1. Place bread in a greased 3- or 4-qt. slow cooker. Combine the next eight ingredients; stir in the cranberries. Pour over bread cubes. Cook, covered, on low until a knife inserted in the center comes out clean, 3-4 hours.

2. For sauce, bring granulated sugar and water to a boil in a large saucepan over medium heat. Cook until the sugar is dissolved and the mixture turns golden amber, about 20 minutes. Gradually stir in cream until smooth. Remove from heat; stir in vanilla. Serve warm with bread pudding. If desired, add a scoop of vanilla ice cream to each serving.

1 SERVING: 479 cal., 23g fat (13g sat. fat), 147mg chol., 237mg sod., 61g carb. (48g sugars, 4g fiber), 9g pro.

CINNAMON-SPICED PUMPKIN FLAN

I love pumpkin and decided to add it to a traditional recipe for flan. It's an interesting change of pace from the usual holiday pie.

—ALISHA RODRIGUES, TETONIA, ID

PREP: 20 MIN. • **BAKE:** 50 MIN. + CHILLING
MAKES: 12 SERVINGS

⅔ **cup sugar**

FLAN

2 **cups half-and-half cream**
6 **large egg yolks**
1 **large egg**
1 **cup sugar**
1 **cup canned pumpkin**
1 **tsp. ground cinnamon**
1 **tsp. vanilla extract**

1. Preheat oven to 325°. In a small heavy saucepan, spread sugar; cook, without stirring, over medium-low heat until it begins to melt. Gently drag melted sugar to center of pan so sugar melts evenly. Cook, without stirring, until the melted sugar turns a medium amber, about 8 minutes. Quickly pour into an ungreased 9-in. deep-dish pie plate, tilting to coat bottom of plate.

2. In a large saucepan, heat cream until bubbles form around side of pan; remove from heat. In a large bowl, whisk egg yolks, egg, sugar, pumpkin, cinnamon and vanilla until blended. Slowly stir in hot cream. Pour into pie plate.

3. Place pie plate in a larger baking pan. Place pan on oven rack; add very hot water to pan to within ½ in. of top of pie plate. Bake 50-60 minutes or until center is just set (mixture will jiggle). Immediately remove flan from water bath to a wire rack; cool 1 hour. Refrigerate until cold, about 5 hours or overnight.

4. Run a knife around edge and invert onto a rimmed serving platter. Refrigerate leftovers.

1 SLICE: 204 cal., 7g fat (4g sat. fat), 128mg chol., 31mg sod., 32g carb. (30g sugars, 1g fiber), 3g pro.

HELPFUL HINT
To make this baked custard into creme brulee instead, omit steps 1 and 4. Bake custard in a broiler-safe dish (or individual ramekins for less time). After cooling, sprinkle sugar over the top(s) and toast with a creme brulee torch or under the broiler until crisp.

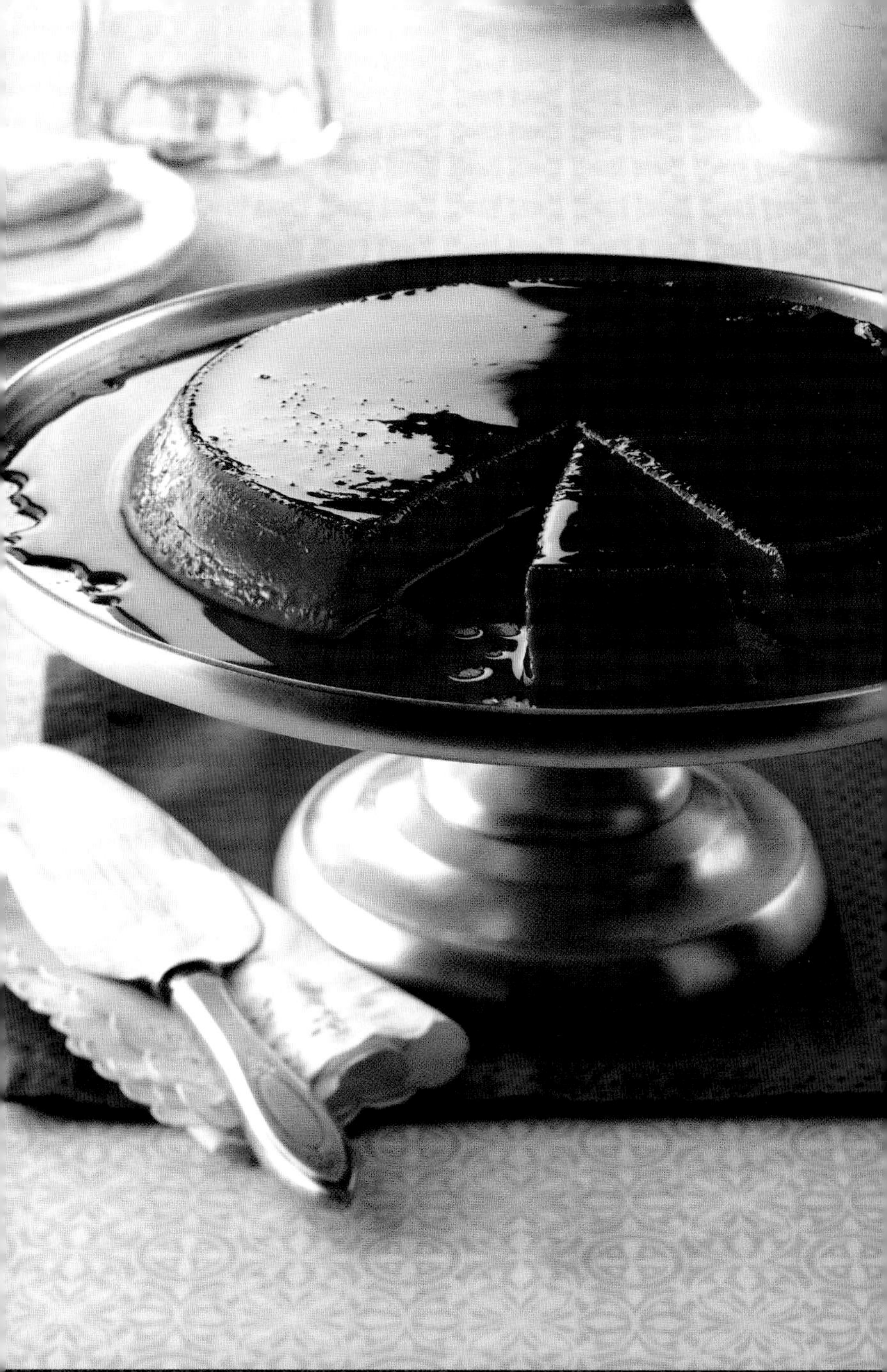

CREAM CHEESE PUMPKIN BARS

The first time I brought these to a church function, there was barely a crumb left on the platter when it was time to leave.
—**KIM CHAMBERS, LAURELTON, NY**

PREP: 25 MIN. • **BAKE:** 35 MIN. + COOLING • **MAKES:** 2 DOZEN

1⅓ cups all-purpose flour
¾ cup sugar, divided
½ cup packed brown sugar
¾ cup cold butter, cubed
1 cup old-fashioned oats
½ cup chopped pecans
1 pkg. (8 oz.) cream cheese, softened, cubed
2 tsp. ground cinnamon
1 tsp. ground allspice
1 tsp. ground cardamom
1 can (15 oz.) solid-pack pumpkin
1 tsp. vanilla extract
3 large eggs, lightly beaten

1. Preheat oven to 350°. In a small bowl, mix flour, ¼ cup sugar and the brown sugar; cut in butter until crumbly. Stir in oats and pecans. Reserve 1 cup for topping.

2. Press the remaining crumb mixture onto the bottom of a greased 13x9-in. baking pan. Bake 15 minutes.

3. In a small bowl, beat cream cheese, spices and remaining sugar until smooth. Beat in pumpkin and vanilla. Add eggs; beat on low speed just until blended. Pour over warm crust; sprinkle with reserved crumb mixture.

4. Bake 20-25 minutes or until a knife inserted in the center comes out clean and filling is set. Cool on a wire rack. Cut into bars. Serve within 2 hours or refrigerate, covered.

1 BAR: 196 cal., 12g fat (6g sat. fat), 52mg chol., 80mg sod., 21g carb. (12g sugars, 1g fiber), 3g pro.

PUMPKIN COOKIES WITH PENUCHE FROSTING

For our parties, we have pumpkin cookies with penuche, a caramel-flavored frosting of brown sugar, butter and milk. We sometimes use home-canned pumpkin.

—PRISCILLA ANDERSON, SALT LAKE CITY, UT

PREP: 25 MIN.
BAKE: 10 MIN./BATCH + COOLING
MAKES: 7 DOZEN

- 1 **cup butter, softened**
- ½ **cup sugar**
- ½ **cup packed brown sugar**
- 1 **large egg**
- 1 **cup canned pumpkin**
- 2 **tsp. vanilla extract**
- 2 **cups all-purpose flour**
- 1 **tsp. baking powder**
- 1 **tsp. baking soda**
- 1 **tsp. ground cinnamon**
- ½ **tsp. salt**
- ¾ **cup chopped pecans**

FROSTING
- ¼ **cup packed brown sugar**
- 3 **Tbsp. butter**
- ¼ **cup 2% milk**
- 2½ **to 3 cups confectioners' sugar**

1. Preheat oven to 350°. In a large bowl, cream butter and sugars until light and fluffy. Beat in egg, pumpkin and vanilla. In another bowl, whisk flour, baking powder, baking soda, cinnamon and salt; gradually beat into creamed mixture. Stir in pecans.

2. Drop cookie dough by rounded teaspoonfuls about 2 in. apart onto ungreased baking sheets. Bake for 9-11 minutes or until edges are light brown. Remove from pans to wire racks to cool completely.

3. For frosting, in a small saucepan, bring brown sugar and butter to a boil. Cook and stir over medium heat 1 minute. Remove from heat; cool 10 minutes. Transfer to a large bowl; beat in milk. Gradually beat in enough confectioners' sugar to achieve spreading consistency. Frost the cookies.

1 COOKIE: 69 cal., 3g fat (2g sat. fat), 9mg chol., 56mg sod., 9g carb. (7g sugars, 0 fiber), 1g pro.

HELPFUL HINT
Cinnamon comes in two basic types: Ceylon and cassia. Ceylon cinnamon's delicate, complex flavor is ideal for ice creams and frostings. The spicy, bolder cassia cinnamon (often labeled simply as cinnamon) is preferred for baking.

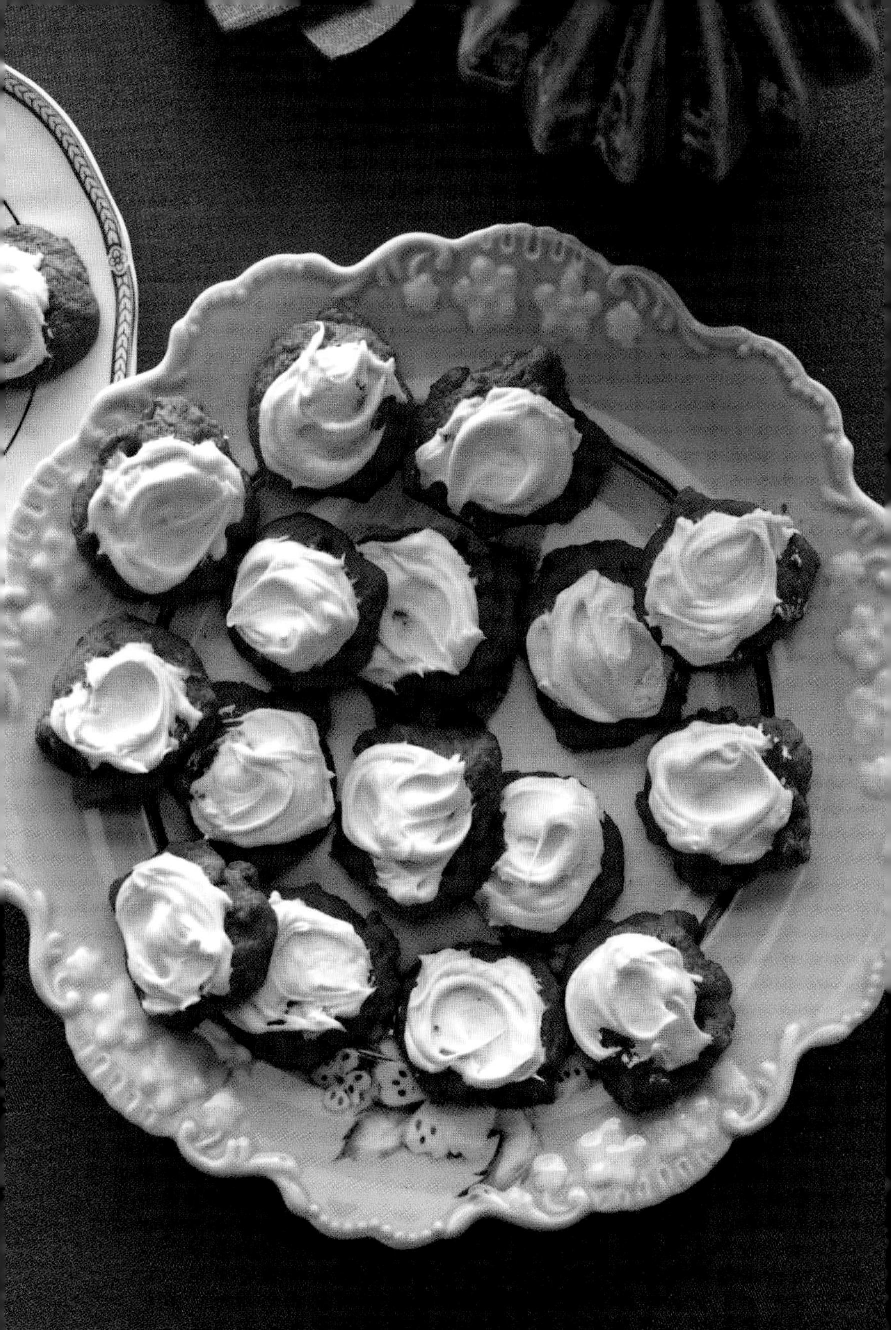

PUMPKIN PIE PUDDING

PREP: 10 MIN. • **COOK:** 6 HOURS
MAKES: 6 SERVINGS

- 1 can (15 oz.) solid-pack pumpkin
- 1 can (12 oz.) evaporated milk
- ¾ cup sugar
- ½ cup biscuit/baking mix
- 2 large eggs, beaten
- 2 Tbsp. butter, melted
- 2½ tsp. pumpkin pie spice
- 2 tsp. vanilla extract
  Sweetened whipped cream or
  vanilla ice cream, optional

1. Combine first eight ingredients.
Transfer to a greased 3-qt. slow cooker.
2. Cook pudding, covered, on low until
a thermometer reads 160°, 6-7 hours. If
desired, serve with whipped or ice cream.

1 SERVING: 229 cal., 9g fat (5g sat. fat), 76mg chol.,
187mg sod., 33g carb. (25g sugars, 2g fiber), 6g pro.

*"My husband loves anything
pumpkin, and this creamy,
comforting dessert is one of
his favorites. We make this
super easy pudding year-
round, but it's especially
nice in fall. "*

—ANDREA SCHAAK, BLOOMINGTON, MN

NOTES

LAYERED PUMPKIN DESSERT

Pretty layers of cheesecake and pumpkin star in this prize-winning torte. Not too heavy, it's especially nice to top off a big meal. There's never a morsel left!

—RUTH ANN STELFOX, RAYMOND, AB

PREP: 40 MIN. + COOLING
BAKE: 15 MIN. + CHILLING
MAKES: 15 SERVINGS

- 1½ cups graham cracker crumbs
- ⅓ cup sugar
- 1 tsp. ground cinnamon
- ⅓ cup butter, melted

CREAM CHEESE FILLING

- 12 oz. cream cheese, softened
- 1 cup sugar
- 3 large eggs

PUMPKIN FILLING

- 1 can (15 oz.) solid-pack pumpkin
- 3 large eggs, separated
- ¾ cup sugar, divided
- ½ cup 2% milk
- 2 tsp. ground cinnamon
- ½ tsp. salt
- 1 envelope unflavored gelatin
- ¼ cup cold water

TOPPING

- 1 cup heavy whipping cream
- 3 Tbsp. sugar
- ¼ tsp. vanilla extract

1. Preheat oven to 350°. In a large bowl, combine crumbs, sugar and cinnamon; stir in butter. Press into an ungreased 13x9-in. baking dish. In a large bowl, beat cream cheese until smooth. Beat in the sugar and eggs until fluffy. Pour over crust. Bake for 15-20 minutes or until set. Cool on a wire rack.

2. In the top of a double boiler or a metal bowl over simmering water, combine pumpkin, egg yolks, ½ cup sugar, milk, cinnamon and salt. Cook and stir mixture over low heat until a thermometer reads 160°; remove from heat. Transfer to a large bowl; wipe out double boiler.

3. In a small saucepan, sprinkle gelatin over cold water; let stand 1 minute. Heat over low heat, stirring until gelatin is completely dissolved. Stir into pumpkin mixture; cool.

4. In the double boiler, whisk egg whites and remaining sugar over low heat until temperature reaches 160°. Remove from heat; using a mixer, beat until stiff glossy peaks form and sugar is dissolved. Fold into pumpkin mixture. Pour over cream cheese layer. Cover and refrigerate for at least 4 hours or until set.

5. Just before serving, in a large bowl, beat cream until it begins to thicken. Add sugar and vanilla; beat until stiff peaks form. Spread over pumpkin layer.

1 PIECE: 370 cal., 21g fat (12g sat. fat), 144mg chol., 275mg sod., 41g carb. (33g sugars, 2g fiber), 6g pro.

HELPFUL HINT

Gelatin cannot be added directly to recipes. It first needs to hydrate, or bloom, in a small amount of liquid and then be heated. Skip this step and you risk problems with texture.

PUMPKIN CHARLOTTE

My mother-in-law gave me this recipe a while back and I just love it! I make it for my husband and his friends during hunting season, and it's always a hit.
—**LORELLE EDGCOMB, GRANVILLE, IL**

PREP: 30 MIN. + CHILLING
MAKES: 12 SERVINGS

- 2 pkg. (3 oz. each) ladyfingers, split
- 6 oz. cream cheese, softened
- 2 Tbsp. sugar
- 2¼ cups heavy whipping cream, divided
- 3 Tbsp. confectioners' sugar, divided
- 1 cup cold whole milk
- 2 pkg. (3.4 oz. each) instant vanilla pudding mix
- ½ tsp. ground cinnamon
- ¼ tsp. ground ginger
- ¼ tsp. pumpkin pie spice
- 1 can (15 oz.) solid-pack pumpkin
  Additional ground cinnamon

1. Split ladyfingers; arrange on the bottom and upright around sides of an ungreased 9-in. springform pan, trimming to fit if necessary. Set aside.

2. In a large bowl, beat cream cheese and sugar until smooth. In a small bowl, beat 1¾ cups whipping cream and 2 Tbsp. confectioners' sugar until stiff peaks form. Set ½ cup aside. Fold remaining whipped cream into the cream cheese mixture. Spread into prepared pan.

3. In a bowl, combine milk, pudding mixes and spices; beat on low speed for 1 minute. Add pumpkin; beat for 1 minute longer. Fold in the reserved whipped cream. Pour over cream cheese layer. Cover and refrigerate for 8 hours or overnight.

4. Just before serving, beat the remaining cream and confectioners' sugar until stiff peaks form. Spoon over pumpkin layer. Sprinkle with cinnamon. Remove sides of pan. Refrigerate leftovers.

1 PIECE: 275 cal., 21g fat (13g sat. fat), 98mg chol., 173mg sod., 21g carb. (16g sugars, 2g fiber), 3g pro.

PUMPKIN PIE BARS

These bars taste like a cross between pumpkin pie and pecan pie. If you can't find butter cake mix, yellow cake mix works.

—SUE DRAHEIM, WATERFORD, WI

PREP: 15 MIN. • **BAKE:** 50 MIN. + CHILLING
MAKES: 16 SERVINGS

- 1 can (29 oz.) solid-pack pumpkin
- 1 can (12 oz.) evaporated milk
- 1½ cups sugar
- 4 large eggs
- 2 tsp. ground cinnamon
- 1 tsp. ground ginger
- ½ tsp. ground nutmeg
- 1 pkg. butter recipe golden cake mix (regular size)
- 1 cup butter, melted
- 1 cup chopped pecans
  Whipped topping, optional

1. Preheat oven to 350°. In a large bowl, combine first seven ingredients; beat on medium speed until smooth. Pour into an ungreased 13x9-in. baking pan. Sprinkle with dry cake mix. Drizzle butter over top; sprinkle with pecans.

2. Bake for 50-60 minutes or until a toothpick inserted in the center comes out clean. Cool for 1 hour on a wire rack.

3. Refrigerate 3 hours or overnight. Remove from refrigerator 15 minutes before serving. Cut into bars. If desired, serve with whipped topping.

1 BAR: 419 cal., 22g fat (10g sat. fat), 91mg chol., 360mg sod., 53g carb. (38g sugars, 3g fiber), 5g pro.

PECAN PUMPKIN PIE PINWHEELS

These pie-like spirals are a pretty way to bring pumpkin flavor to dessert any time of the year.

—KATHY YAROSH, APOPKA, FL

PREP: 45 MIN. + CHILLING
BAKE: 20 MIN./BATCH + COOLING
MAKES: 4 DOZEN

- 1½ cups solid-pack pumpkin
- ½ cup sweetened shredded coconut
- ½ cup finely chopped pecans
- ¼ cup packed brown sugar
- 1 tsp. ground cinnamon
- 1 tsp. pumpkin pie spice
- 1 pkg. (11 oz.) pie crust mix
- ½ cup cream cheese frosting
- 1 to 2 tsp. 2% milk

1. In a small bowl, combine the first six ingredients. Prepare pie crust mix according to package directions; divide dough in half.

2. Roll each portion into a 14x8-in. rectangle on lightly floured pieces of waxed paper. Spread half of pumpkin mixture over one rectangle to within ¼ in. of edges. Roll up tightly jelly-roll style, starting with a long side. Wrap in waxed paper. Repeat with the remaining dough. Freeze 30 minutes or until firm.

3. Preheat oven to 400°. Using a sharp serrated knife, trim ends and cut the dough crosswise into ¼-in. slices. Place 1 in. apart on parchment paper-lined baking sheets. Bake for 18-22 minutes or until light golden. Remove from pans to wire racks to cool completely.

4. In a small bowl, combine frosting and enough milk to reach a drizzling consistency. Drizzle over pinwheels and let stand until set. Store cookies between pieces of waxed paper in airtight containers.

FREEZE OPTION Place wrapped logs in a resealable plastic freezer bag; return to freezer. To use, unwrap frozen logs and cut into slices. If necessary, let the dough stand for 15 minutes at room temperature before cutting. Bake as directed, increasing time by 2-4 minutes.

1 COOKIE: 67 cal., 4g fat (2g sat. fat), 0 chol., 55mg sod., 7g carb. (3g sugars, 0 fiber), 1g pro.

HELPFUL HINT

Slice-and-bake cookies are great to keep on hand for unexpected guests. Just pull the dough from the freezer, slice off the desired number of cookies and bake. For a last-minute touch, drizzle with an icing of confectioners' sugar and milk, or lightly dust with confectioners' sugar.

MINI PUMPKIN CUSTARDS

Dinner guests don't need to feel guilty about indulging in dessert when they're offered small cups of this creamy custard. Each spoonful is like pumpkin pie without the calorie-laden crust.

—LESLIE TRIPP, NORTH POTOMAC, MD

PREP: 25 MIN. • **BAKE:** 20 MIN. + CHILLING • **MAKES:** 8 SERVINGS

- ½ cup half-and-half cream
- ½ cup heavy whipping cream
- 3 large egg yolks
- 2 Tbsp. plus 2 tsp. sugar
- ⅛ tsp. ground cinnamon
  Dash each salt, ground cloves and nutmeg
- ⅓ cup canned pumpkin
- ¼ cup maple syrup
- ½ tsp. vanilla extract
  Whipped cream and additional ground nutmeg

1. In a small saucepan, heat half-and-half and heavy cream until bubbles form around sides of pan. In a small bowl, whisk egg yolks, sugar, cinnamon, salt, cloves and nutmeg.

2. Remove cream from the heat; stir a small amount of hot cream into the egg mixture. Return all to the pan, stirring constantly. Stir in the pumpkin, syrup and vanilla.

3. Transfer mixture to eight stoneware demitasse cups or 2-oz. ramekins. Place cups in a baking pan; add 1 in. boiling water to the pan.

4. Bake, uncovered, at 325° for 25-30 minutes for demitasse cups and 20-25 minutes for ramekins or until centers are just set (custards will jiggle). Remove cups from water bath; cool for 10 minutes. Cover and refrigerate at least 4 hours. Garnish with whipped cream and additional nutmeg.

1 SERVING: 138 cal., 9g fat (5g sat. fat), 105mg chol., 36mg sod., 13g carb. (11g sugars, 0 fiber), 2g pro. **DIABETIC EXCHANGES:** 1 starch, 1 fat.

PUMPKIN WHOOPIE PIES

My kids start begging me for these cakelike sandwich cookies as soon as autumn arrives. I haven't met a person yet who doesn't like these fun little treats.

—DEB STUBER, CARLISLE, PA

PREP: 30 MIN. + CHILLING
BAKE: 10 MIN./BATCH + COOLING
MAKES: 2 DOZEN

- 1 **cup shortening**
- 2 **cups packed brown sugar**
- 2 **large eggs**
- 1 **tsp. vanilla extract**
- 3½ **cups all-purpose flour**
- 1½ **tsp. baking powder**
- 1½ **tsp. baking soda**
- 1 **tsp. salt**
- 1 **tsp. ground cinnamon**
- 1 **tsp. ground ginger**
- 1½ **cups canned pumpkin**

FILLING

- ¼ **cup all-purpose flour**
  Dash salt
- ¾ **cup whole milk**
- 1 **cup shortening**
- 2 **cups confectioners' sugar**
- 2 **tsp. vanilla extract**

1. Preheat oven to 400°. Cream shortening and brown sugar until light and fluffy. Add the eggs, one at a time, beating well after each addition. Beat in vanilla. In another bowl, whisk next six ingredients; beat into the creamed mixture alternately with pumpkin.

2. Drop by rounded tablespoonfuls 2 in. apart onto greased baking sheets; flatten slightly with the back of a spoon. Bake for 10-11 minutes. Remove to wire racks to cool.

3. For filling, combine the flour and salt in a small saucepan. Gradually whisk in the milk until smooth; bring to a boil over medium-high heat. Reduce the heat to medium; cook and stir until thickened, about 2 minutes. Refrigerate mixture, covered, until completely cooled.

4. In another bowl, beat shortening, confectioners' sugar and vanilla until smooth. Add chilled milk mixture; beat until light and fluffy, about 7 minutes. Spread on the bottoms of half of the cookies; cover with remaining cookies. Store whoopie pies in the refrigerator.

1 SANDWICH COOKIE: 344 cal., 17g fat (4g sat. fat), 16mg chol., 284mg sod., 45g carb. (29g sugars, 1g fiber), 3g pro.

FROZEN PUMPKIN MOUSSE PARFAITS

Even people who don't care for pumpkin pie rave about these frosty parfaits. The creamy mousse contrasts wonderfully with the nutty toffee crunch pieces.

—JANE LISKA, HARBOR SPRINGS, MI

PREP: 35 MIN. + FREEZING
MAKES: 8 SERVINGS

- 1 **cup chopped walnuts**
- 1 **cup brickle toffee bits**
- 1 **Tbsp. brown sugar**
- 1 **Tbsp. butter, melted**

MOUSSE

- 3½ **cups heavy whipping cream, divided**
- 2 **cups sugar**
- 10 **large egg yolks, beaten**
- 2 **cans (15 oz. each) solid-pack pumpkin**
- ¼ **cup dark rum or 2 tsp. rum extract**
- 2 **tsp. ground cinnamon**
- 2 **tsp. vanilla extract**
- 1 **tsp. ground ginger**
- ½ **tsp. salt**
- ½ **tsp. ground nutmeg**

1. In a small bowl, combine the walnuts, toffee bits, brown sugar and butter. Press into a thin layer on a greased baking sheet. Bake at 350° for 10-13 minutes or until golden brown. Cool. Break into small pieces.

2. In a large saucepan, combine 1½ cups whipping cream and sugar. Cook and stir over medium heat for 10-15 minutes or until slightly thickened. Remove from the heat.

3. Stir a small amount of hot mixture into egg yolks; return all to the pan, stirring constantly. Bring to a gentle boil; cook and stir 2 minutes longer. Remove from the heat. Stir in the pumpkin, rum, cinnamon, vanilla, ginger, salt and nutmeg. Transfer to a large bowl. Cool mixture to room temperature without stirring. Press waxed paper onto surface of the pudding; refrigerate until chilled.

4. In a small bowl, beat 1 cup cream until stiff peaks form. Fold into the pumpkin mixture.

5. In each of eight dessert dishes, layer 4 tsp. walnut mixture and ½ cup mousse; repeat layers. Freeze for at least 3 hours or overnight.

6. Just before serving, in a small bowl, beat the remaining cream until stiff peaks form. Garnish the parfaits with whipped cream and the remaining walnut mixture.

1 PARFAIT: 952 cal., 66g fat (32g sat. fat), 412mg chol., 383mg sod., 84g carb. (74g sugars, 6g fiber), 10g pro.

RECIPE INDEX